THE FIRST ENGLISHMEN IN INDIA

D1830595

THE FIRST ENGLISHMEN IN INDIA

LETTERS AND NARRATIVES OF SUNDRY ELIZABETHANS WRITTEN BY THEMSEL VES AND EDITED WITH AN INTRODUCTION AND NOTES BY

J. COURTENAY LOCKE

GYAN

Published by

Gyan Publishing House
5, Ansari Road
Daryaganj, New Delhi-110002
Phone: 011-47034999, 9811692060
E-mail: books@gyanbooks.com

Distribution Network
gyanbooks.com
India, USA, Canada, UK, Australia, France

© **Publisher**
All rights reserved. No part of this work may be reproduced, stored, adapted, or transmitted in any form or by any means, electronic, mechanical, photocopying, micro-filming, recording or otherwise, or translated in any language, without the prior written permission of the copyright owner and the publisher.

ISBN : 978-81-212-2378-2 (PB)
First Published, 1930

2nd Impression 2021

Printed at: Gyan Press, Delhi.

The book is sold subject to the condition that it shall not, by way of trade or otherwise, be lent, resold, hired out, or otherwise circulated without the prior publisher's written consent.

The
First Englishmen in India
Author: J. Courtenay Locke

THE BROADWAY TRAVELLERS

EDITED BY SIR E. DENISON ROSS
AND EILEEN POWER

THE FIRST ENGLISHMEN IN INDIA

Letters and Narratives of sundry Elizabethans written by themselves and edited with an Introduction and Notes by

J. COURTENAY LOCKE

Published by

GEORGE ROUTLEDGE & SONS, LTD.

BROADWAY HOUSE, CARTER LANE, LONDON

JOHN ELDRED

[front.

PREFACE

THE text of Newbery's letters to Hareborne of July 15th and August 15th, 1583; Eldred's letter to Hareborne of July 14th, 1583, and Eldred and Shales' letters to Hareborne of November 6th, 1583, and January 22nd, 1584, is that of the 1905 MacLehose edition of "Purchas his Pilgrimes"; all the rest of the text is from the 1903 MacLehose edition of Hakluyt. In each case comparison has been made with the 1625 edition of Purchas and both the 1589 and 1598 editions of Hakluyt where comparison seemed needful; the results of the comparison will be found in the notes.

The spelling has been modernised throughout except where a real inflection is involved, as with "merchandises", for instance, or where the retention of an old spelling has some philological excuse, remarked in the notes. In the case of "swarveth" I am afraid this excuse is of the slightest and I have to confess that I retained the spelling because I liked it. The original spelling of place-names, with variants, has been retained, except in the case of Ormus, where it was not thought worth while to disturb uniformity for the sake of an occasional erratic final "z". Foreign personal names remain unaltered in every case; the English have been kept to their accepted modern forms.

The separate items have been collected into a whole and the various letters inserted as neatly as possible in their proper chronological places; the punctuation, also, has been rendered as orderly as possible and the cumbersome paragraphs divided into more wieldy lengths; otherwise the text has not been tampered with in any way.

To save the annoyance of merely negative notes it will be convenient to express here my regret at being unable to furnish any elucidation whatever of Serrion and Selwy, although I feel they are really quite easy. They await the attention of more fortunate investigators.

I make my acknowledgments to the monumental issues of the Hakluyt Society and to the exhaustless Yule—equally indispensable to all workers in this field. To a previous modern edition of one of the items I regret that it is unexpectedly impossible to make any acknowledgment.

J. Courtenay Locke.

CONTENTS

	PAGE
PLACE-NAMES IN TABLE OF JOURNEYS	x
TABLE OF JOURNEYS	xi
INTRODUCTION	1
STEVENS, LETTER TO HIS FATHER, 10TH NOVEMBER, 1579 .	19
QUEEN ELIZABETH, LETTER TO ZELABDIM ECHEBAR, FEBRUARY, 1583	31
QUEEN ELIZABETH, LETTER TO KING OF CHINA, FEBRUARY, 1583	32
ELDRED, RELATION	34
NEWBERY, LETTER TO HAKLUYT, 28TH MAY, 1583 . .	37
NEWBERY, LETTER TO POORE, 29TH MAY, 1583 . . .	39
ELDRED, RELATION	43
ELDRED, LETTER TO G. S., 14TH JULY, 1583 . . .	47
NEWBERY, LETTER TO HAREBORNE, 15TH JULY, 1583 . .	50
NEWBERY, LETTER TO POORE, 20TH JULY, 1583 . . .	52
NEWBERY, LETTER TO HAREBORNE, 15TH AUGUST, 1583 .	54
ELDRED, RELATION	57
NEWBERY, LETTER TO ELDRED AND SHALES, 21ST SEPTEMBER, 1583	59
NEWBERY, LETTER TO ELDRED AND SHALES, 24TH SEPTEMBER, 1583	61
ELDRED AND SHALES, LETTER TO G. S., 6TH NOVEMBER, 1583 .	61

CONTENTS

PAGE

Eldred and Shales, Letter to G. S., 22nd January, 1584 . . . 64

Eldred, Relation 66

Fitch, Relation 69

Newbery, Letter to Poore, 20th January, 1584 . . . 79

Fitch, Letter to Poore, 25th January, 1584. . . . 85

Fitch, Relation 88

Linschoten, Report 89

Fitch, Relation 99

Frey Peter, Letter to Frey Diego, 28th December, 1589 150

Index 219

LIST OF ILLUSTRATIONS

JOHN ELDRED . . . . *Frontispiece*

From a photograph of the portrait-bust on his Memorial Tablet in the Church at Great Saxham, Suffolk.

PAGE

VIEW OF LISBON ABOUT 1570 20

From Braun and Hohenberg, *Théâtre des cités du monde*, 1574–1617.

VIEW OF TRIPOLI ABOUT 1610 36

From the *Relation journalière du voyage du Levant* of Henri de Beauvau, 1615.

THE ISLAND AND TOWN OF ORMUS 74

From an old engraving.

GOA MARKET-PLACE 78

From *Voyages into the East*, J. H. van Linschoten, 1598.

CIVIL AND MILITARY COSTUMES OF THE PORTUGUESE IN GOA . 94

From Linschoten's *Voyages*, as above.

PORTUGUESE SOLDIER TAKING HIS PLEASURE IN A PALANQUIN . . 120

From Linschoten's *Voyages*, as above.

THE PEARL-FISHERY AT TUTICORIN ON THE TINNEVELLI COAST. 148

From an old plate illustrating Jan Nieuhof's Indian voyages, 1653–1662.

MAPS

THE TERRITORY OF GOA xvi

FITCH'S ROUTES BETWEEN TRIPOLIS AND ORMUZ, OUT AND HOME 60

FITCH'S INDIAN VOYAGES AND JOURNEYS. 138

ALPHABETICAL LIST

Of Place-names in Table of Journeys

Text Form	Modern Form
Agulias, Cape das	*Agulhas, Cape.*
Babylon . . .	*Baghdad.*
Bacola . . .	*Barisal.*
Balsara . . .	*Basra.*
Bannaras . .	*Benares.*
Barrampore . .	*Burhanpur.*
Basaim . . .	*Bassein.*
Bellapore . . .	*Balapur.*
Bellergan . .	*Belgaum.*
Birrah . . .	*Birejik.*
Bisapor . . .	*Bijapur.*
Canarian Isles .	*Canary Islands.*
Chatigan . . .	*Chittagong.*
Cosmin . . .	*Bassein.*
Couche . . .	*Kuch Behar.*
Cyrion . . .	*Syriam (Thanlyeng).*
Dela	*Dala.*
Fatepore . . .	*Fatehpur Sikri.*
Felugia . . .	*Fellujah.*
Gulconda . . .	*Golconda.*
Hammah . . .	*Hamah.*
Hugeli . . .	*Hugli.*
Jamahey . . .	*Zimmé (Chieng-Mai).*
Macao . . .	*Mayet-kyi.*
Mandoway . .	*Mandu (Mandogarh).*
Medon . . .	*Myaungmya.*
Merdin . . .	*Mardin.*
Orfa	*Urfah.*
Ormus . . .	*Hormuz.*
Patenaw . . .	*Patna.*
Prage . . .	*Allahabad.*
Satagam . . .	*Satgaon.*
Serrepore . .	*Sripur.*
Serringe . . .	*Sironj.*
Servidore . .	*Bidar.*
Tana	*Thana.*
Tripolis . . .	*Tripoli.*
Ugini	*Ujjain.*
Zocotoro . . .	*Socotra.*

TABLE OF JOURNEYS

Place-names spelt as they first appear in Text. Distances approximate only. The references in brackets are to the pages in text where arrivals and departures are first indicated. Dates are given exactly if text shows them; where estimated or altogether doubtful they are followed or replaced by marks of interrogation. To facilitate reference while avoiding a crowded Table, names appearing in an old spelling are given in alphabetical order above followed by their modern equivalents, with alternatives to the latter (if any) in brackets.

STEVENS

Leaves—				*Arrives at—*				Miles
				Lisbon	*28th March,*	*1579*	(p. 19)	
Lisbon	*4th April,*	*1579*	(p. 19)	*Porto Santo*	*10th April,*	,,	(p. 20)	595
Porto Santo	*10th* ,,	,,	(p. 20)	*Canarian Isles*	*13th* ,,	,,	(p. 20)	250
Canarian Isles	*17th* (?) ,,	,,	(p. 20)	*The Equator*	*30th May,*	,,	(p. 21)	2,500
The Equator	*30th May,*	,,	(p. 21)	*Cape das Agulias*	*29th July,*	,,	(p. 26)	3,300
Cape das Agulias	*30th July,*	,,	(p. 27)	*Zocotoro*	*14th* (?) October,	,,	(p. 29)	5,000
Zocotoro	*14th* (?) October,	,,	(p. 29)	*Goa*	*24th* ,,	,,	(p. 30)	1,150

ELDRED, NEWBERY, FITCH, LEEDES, STORY

Leave—				*Arrive at—*				Miles
London	*12th February,*	*1583*	(p. 34)	*Gravesend*	*12th February,*	*1583*	(p. 37)	30
Gravesend	*13th* ,,	,,	(p. 37)	*The Downs, off Deal*	*25th (?)* ,,	,,	(p. 40)	75
Deal	*25th* ,,	,,	(p. 40)	*Falmouth*	*11th March,*	,,	(p. 38)	340
Falmouth	*11th March,*	,,	(p. 38)	*Tripolis*	*1st May,*	,,	(p. 34)	3,700
Tripolis	*14th May,*	,,	(p. 36)	*Hammah*	*17th (?) May,*	,,	(p. 36)	100
Hammah	*18th (?) May,*	,,	(p. 36)	*Aleppo*	*21st May,*	,,	(p. 37)	80
Aleppo	*31st May,*	,,	(p. 43)	*Birrah*	*2nd June,*	,,	(p. 43)	80
Birrah	*2nd June,*	,,	(p. 43)	*Felugia*	*28th* ,,	,,	(p. 45)	600
Felugia	*5th (?) July,*	,,	(p. 45)	*Babylon*	*6th (?) July,*	,,	(p. 45)	40
Babylon	*27th June,*	,,	(p. 54)	*Balsara*	*6th August,*	,,	(p. 54)	400

Here Eldred and the others finally parted company. From Basra, Newbery, Fitch, Leedes and Story proceeded as appears below, while Eldred returned, leaving Basra about the 6th February, 1584, arriving at Baghdad about the 22nd March and at Aleppo, passing by Hit, about the 11th June. From Aleppo he journeyed to and from Baghdad twice and then to Antioch, Tripoli, Joppa, Rama, Lycia, Gaza, Jerusalem, Bethlehem and other places of Palestine, and back to Joppa and Tripoli, which he finally left in the ship "Hercules" on the 22nd December, 1587, reaching London once more on the 26th March, 1588.

NEWBERY, FITCH, LEEDES AND STORY

Leave—				Arrive at—				Miles
Balsara	20th (?) August,	1583	(p. 86)	Ormus	4th September,	1583	(p. 59)	700
Ormus	11th October,	„	(p. 75)	Diu	5th November,	„	(p. 75)	1,200
Diu	5th (?) November,	„	(p. 76)	Daman	7th (?) „	„	(p. 76)	120
Daman	7th (?) „	„	(p. 76)	Basaim	9th (?) „	„	(p. 76)	120
Basaim	9th (?) „	„	(p. 76)	Tana	9th (?) „	„	(p. 76)	20
Tana	9th (?) „	„	(p. 76)	Chaul	10th „	„	(p. 76)	50
Chaul	20th (?) „	„	(p. 86)	Goa	29th „	„	(p. 86)	260

NEWBERY, FITCH AND LEEDES

Leave—				Arrive at—				
Goa	5th April,	1585	(p. 89)	Bellergan	April (?)	1585	(p. 99)	60
Bellergan	„ (?)	„	(p. 99)	Bisapor	„ (?)	„	(p. 99)	100
Bisapor	„ (?)	„	(p. 100)	Gulconda	„ (?)	„	(p. 100)	200
Gulconda	May (?)	„	(p. 100)	Servidore	May (?)	„	(p. 100)	120
Servidore	„ (?)	„	(p. 101)	Bellapore	„ (?)	„	(p. 101)	120
Bellapore	„ (?)	„	(p. 101)	Barrampore	„ (?)	„	(p. 101)	50
Barrampore	„ (?)	„	(p. 102)	Mandoway	June (?)	„	(p. 102)	90
Mandoway	June (?)	„	(p. 102)	Ugini	„ (?)	„	(p. 102)	70
Ugini	„ (?)	„	(p. 102)	Serringe	„ (?)	„	(p. 102)	140
Serringe	„ (?)	„	(p. 102)	Agra	July (?)	„	(p. 102)	220
Agra	July (?)	„	(p. 102)	Fatepore	„ (?)	„	(p. 102)	23

FITCH

Leaves—				Arrives at—				Miles
Fatepore	October (?)	1585	(p. 104)	Agra	October (?)	1585	(p. 104)	23
Agra	,, (?)	,,	(p. 104)	Prage	November (?)	,,	(p. 106)	350
Prage	November (?)	,,	(p. 106)	Bannaras	December (?)	,,	(p. 107)	120
Bannaras	December (?)	,,	(p. 112)	Patenaw	January (?)	1586	(p. 112)	200
Patenaw	January (?)	1586	(p. 113)	Tanda	February (?)	,,	(p. 113)	260
Tanda	February (?)	,,	(p. 114)	Couche	March (?)	,,	(p. 114)	130
Couche	March (?)	,,	(p. 115)	Hugeli	April (?)	,,	(p. 115)	250
Hugeli	May (?)	,,	(p. 115)	Satagam	May (?)	,,	(p. 115)	3
Satagam	July (?)	,,	(p. 117)	Chatigan	August (?)	,,	(p. 117)	270
Chatigan	August (?)	,,	(p. 118)	Bacola	September (?)	,,	(p. 118)	150
Bacola	September (?)	,,	(p. 119)	Serrepore	October (?)	,,	(p. 119)	50
Serrepore	28th November	,,	(p. 119)	Negrais	5th (?) December,	,,	(p. 120)	600
Negrais	6th (?) December	,,	(p. 120)	Cosmin	9th (?) ,,	,,	(p. 120)	80
Cosmin	9th (?) ,,	,,	(p. 120)	Medon	10th (?) ,,	,,	(p. 121)	40
Medon	10th (?) ,,	,,	(p. 121)	Dela	11th (?) ,,	,,	(p. 121)	50
Dela	12th (?) ,,	,,	(p. 121)	Cirion	14th (?) ,,	,,	(p. 121)	90
Cirion	15th (?) ,,	,,	(p. 121)	Macao	15th (?) ,,	,,	(p. 121)	20
Macao	16th (?) ,,	,,	(p. 121)	Pegu	16th (?) ,,	,,	(p. 121)	30
Pegu	?	?	(p. 134)	Jamahey	?	?	(p. 134)	280
Jamahey	?	?	(p. 136)	Pegu	?	?	(p. 136)	280
Pegu	10th January,	1587(?)	(p. 138)	Malacca	8th February,	1587(?)	(p. 138)	1,300
Malacca	29th March,	1588	(p. 141)	Pegu	27th (?) April,	1588	(p. 141)	1,300
Pegu	17th September,	,,	(p. 141)	Cosmin	24th (?) September,	,,	(p. 141)	230
Cosmin	October (?)	,,	(p. 141)	Bengal	November (?)	,,	(p. 142)	600

Bengal	*3rd February,*	1589	(p. 142)	*Ceylon*	*6th March,*	1589	(p. 142)	1,500
Ceylon	*11th March,*	"	(p. 144)	*Cochin*	*22nd "*	"	(p. 144)	350
Cochin	*2nd November,*	"	(p. 146)	*Goa*	*10th (?) November,*	"	(p. 146)	400
Goa	*13th (?) "*	"	(p. 146)	*Chaul*	*18th (?) "*	"	(p. 146)	240
Chaul	*11th (?) December,*	"	(p. 147)	*Ormus*	*7th (?) January,*	1590	(p. 147)	1,200
Ormus	*26th (?) February,*	1590	(p. 149)	*Balsara*	*20th (?) March,*	"	(p. 149)	700
Balsara	?	"	(p. 149)	*Babylon*	?	"	(p. 149)	400
Babylon	?	"	(p. 149)	*Mosul*	?	"	(p. 149)	200
Mosul	?	"	(p. 149)	*Merdin*	?	"	(p. 149)	150
Merdin	?	"	(p. 149)	*Orfa*	?	"	(p. 149)	100
Orfa	?	"	(p. 149)	*Birrah*	?	"	(p. 149)	50
Birrah	*January (?)*	1591	(p. 149)	*Aleppo*	*January (?)*	1591	(p. 149)	80
Aleppo	*" (?)*	"	(p. 149)	*Tripolis*	*February (?)*	"	(p. 149)	180
Tripolis	*12th (?) February,*	"	(p. 149)	*London*	*29th April,*	"	(p. 149)	4,100

See page X for Alphabetical List of Place-names in above Table, showing text and modern forms.

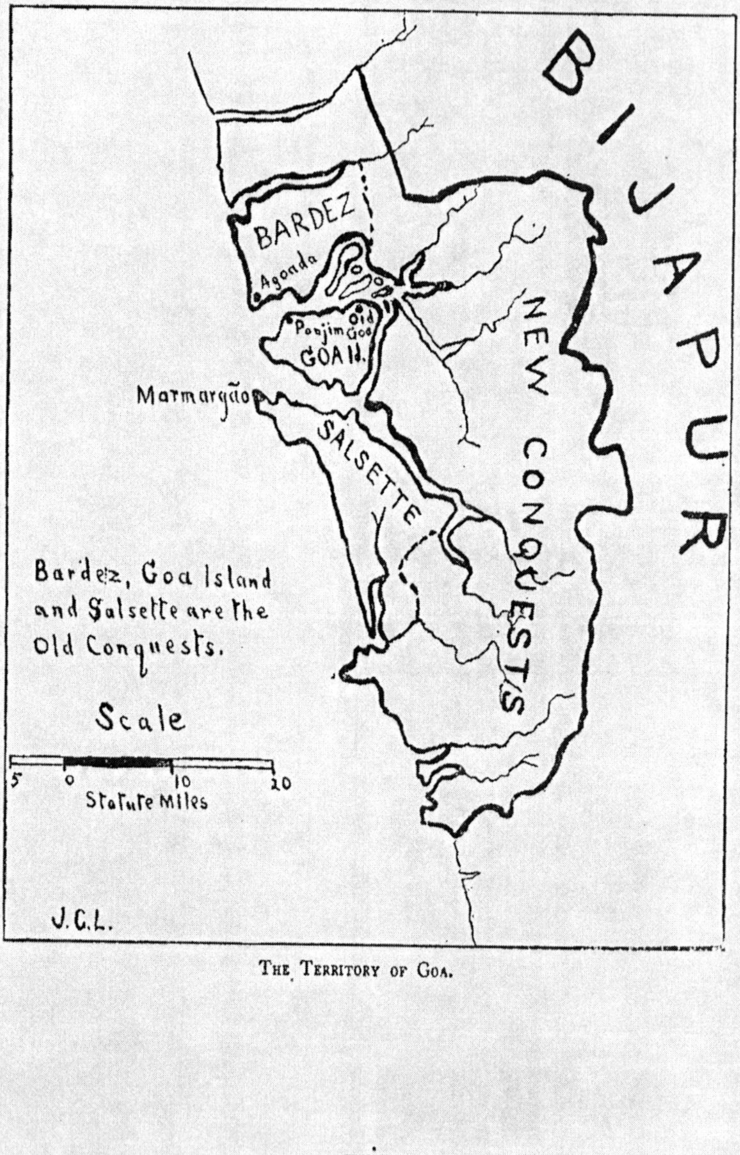

THE TERRITORY OF GOA.

INTRODUCTION

APART from the fact that for those with the palate for their reserved flavour they make very good reading, the narrations and letters which follow present a matter so important as the beginnings of our empire in India. That the vast phenomenon presented to our minds when the word is spelt with a capital initial and called "Empire" should grow out of the spying-adventure of two merchant-companions is an astonishing piece of evolution. That it should grow, in immediate fact, out of the operations of the East India Company—so purely a trading concern; so earnestly reluctant to consider any imperial idea; so heavily oppressed in its corporate mind by the mere thought of Empire and all its uneconomic splendours—may be not the least surprising part of the whole business, but that is a well-known story. Surprising matters enough, and our present concern, are how the Company grew out of the adventure and the kind of circumstances with which the adventure was surrounded.

Our stage is set in 1583. England was then thriving, but her prosperity was burdened with the army of sturdy beggars and other indigent folk which was to cause the remedial Poor Law measures culminating in 1601. Her only industry of commanding magnitude was the cloth-trade ; her only present means of attaining a more diffused prosperity was by finding fresh markets for her cloth and by trade generally ; the only ready markets to be seen lay in countries of which other nations held the gate, and those countries were mainly the Levant and what lay eastward and south-westward of it, and especially India.

The discovery of America is to us so much the most sensational geographical fact of that age that it needs a fairly considerable readjustment of our ideas to realise that to the Elizabethan merchant it had for some time been a fact with no flavour of sensation. America, as we know well, had in any case been discovered in a search not for America but for a new road to India. With the realisation that this new part of the earth was really new came a multitude of new and exciting curiosities concerning it, but in these the share of the merchant-mind was a desire to know what America was good for in the way of trade. A new road to India it clearly was not ; rather a new wall across any such road, with Spain on the ramparts instead of Portugal, Venice and the Turk, as on the Eastward wall. If any brave Frobisher or Willoughby could find some way round by means of a North-west Passage or otherwise the merchant was prepared to be greatly interested once more, and meanwhile would help reasonably with money towards the finding; if hot-headed adventurers chose to go in for piracy on the American coasts or sea-roads them also he would help discreetly with money, taking his share of whatever pickings there might be; if enthusiasts proposed to colonise the new-found lands the merchant, not addicted to enthusiasms then or since, would lend them little more than a most unready ear: it is familiar to us that America was colonised through political and religious repression rather than commercial expansion. For the rest, he would remember that he bore Spain a grudge for denying him the freedom of such trade as there was, but he had no pressing instant interest in the matter since the trade appeared to be meagre except for gold, silver and slaves. The slaves were attended to by Bristol for what they were worth. The gold and silver, thanks to the lofty methods of Spain, flowed refreshingly over the rest of Europe in payment for the commodities she disdained to produce herself, and left Spain, the mere conduit, ultimately dry and barren. The English merchant found he was getting a fair share of refreshment by his accustomed ways of trade and hoped to get more as his trade increased, so, freed of anxiety, he turned considering eyes to the East as of old.

INTRODUCTION

The East was still the fountain of all richness. Gold, silver, pearls, dyes; precious stuffs and stones and spices almost as precious—of these and much more there was no end to what she gave. The excessive spice-hunger of those days sometimes seems strange to us until we remember our consumption of tea, and anyway we can get all the spices we want for an old song. But the Elizabethans lived on salt meat from autumn to spring; their fresh meat was of poor quality in general; for the good of the fisherman the Law compelled them to eat fish more often than they cared about, and with all this insipid food their craving for pungent flavourings was probably and naturally much stronger than ours. They liked heavily-spiced drinks, moreover, for they had no tea.

However to be explained, this desire for spices and the difficulty of obtaining them was a chief factor in the jealous contest for the road to India and was long to remain so. The Venetian hold of that road had lasted long but was now relaxing, though Venice still lay firmly entrenched along the routes through Syria, from Aleppo across to Baghdad and down to Basra. The Portuguese held the new sea-road round the Cape, and their citadel at Hormuz closed the outlet from Basra through the Persian Gulf. And between them Venice and Portugal doled out spices to the resentful markets of Europe in the quantities and at the prices they chose.

So the English merchant kept his eye steady and covetous on the East, but there was no free road for him. The sea-way was as yet, from a commercial point of view, all but impossible. Stevens' letter shows something of what it meant even to the Portuguese. Since the days of Henry the Navigator, a hundred and fifty years before, they had been desperately acquiring and accumulating the secrets of that road. They knew every sea-sign of it; they had their own friendly stations spaced all along it; they travelled it in companies of great ships, equipped according to the lessons of their long experience and furnished with all that was then possible of sailing-directions, rules of pilotage and charts, and in spite of all they were lucky if they could "go it," as Stevens says, in five months from Lisbon to Goa, with a third or fourth of their companies rotting with scurvy and many dead of it. The English ships, though weatherly and heavily gunned, were small: if food and water failed, as they often did when they kept the sea for any length of time, it was chance work replenishing them; every port was armed and hostile; every ship they met was an enemy and had to be fought or run from (but the English seldom ran); to reach India was to sail into a nest of wasps; they sailed as poachers and pirates and so were without the Law, and the navigation was all sheer guess-work.

Richard Hakluyt had been for years at work trying to build up some English School of Navigation, and we know how he dealt with every scrap of seafaring news. Stevens' letter was one of his interceptions (perhaps his friend Walsingham let him have it) and that helped a little. Other papers from captured Spanish and Portuguese ships were to come to his hands by degrees and in time provide knowledge enough for the long voyage, but that was not yet. The Levant road must be the way.

The English had traded to the Levant throughout the sixteenth century, but only in a very small way until 1550. With Bodenham's voyage in that year greater activity began, and at last by 1578 Osborne and Staper had extracted a safe-conduct from the Turkish Sultan for their factor, William Hareborne, whom they sent out to use it in Constantinople in 1578, and who used it so well that—to make short—Elizabeth in 1581 saw that it was good to grant private letters-patent to Osborne and Staper and their chosen merchant-associates no more than twelve in number to trade into the dominions of the Grand Turk, to the exclusion of all not patented. So the Osborne and Staper ships began to sail briskly, and by 1583 there was a fairly sound trade, an English consul at Aleppo, and a foothold firm enough to think of going further.

The Levant voyage, through a Mediterranean infested with the pirate-galleys of every Mohammadan breed, was dangerous, but English seamen were growing used to its dangers and learning to meet them effectively. The land journey to Basra from the Levant ports held dangers as great, though more subtle, in the varied forms of disease, quiet murder and a blasting climate, and the difficulties were far greater. Every step of the road had to be forced against defrauding Turks, blackmailing Arabs or stealthily obstructing Venetians. These matters also had been dealt with by the English merchant. His scouting parties, sparse but far-flung, had roughly surveyed Mesopotamia and the country from Persia to the Egyptian seaboard, and with the working knowledge slowly and painfully gained he had thrust doggedly south until Basra and some scanty footing in it were attained. Only the next step—from Basra to India—remained, but that was into the unknown.

Portugal held the Persian Gulf and every European gate into India, and since 1580—loosely enough—Portugal was held by Spain, who might be secretly flouted but was not yet to be openly defied. The English were well used to going their ways unperturbed by Portugal or Spain or both of them, so in 1583 the last step was to be taken.

Osborne and Staper fitted out the famous *Tiger*, gave her a chosen cargo, and set in her a company of picked merchants. Of those who mostly concern us, John Eldred knew the route from Aleppo to Baghdad very well and had lived in Baghdad altogether more than two years; John Newbery spoke Arabic and had voyaged to Tripoli and Syria in March 1578, returning in November 1579, and again in September 1580, returning in August 1582; the second time he had reached Basra, Persia and Hormuz. These two were, clearly, seasoned and prepared men. The third, Ralph Fitch (in the end the most remarkable), is not known to us before this time. A merchant he certainly was, and that is all we can be sure about—except that no mistake was made in choosing him. Cool, bold, contented, good-humoured and patient of hardship it is easy to read him. Fertile in wise devices he must have been, for he had no Arabic, even, to start with and only his share of what money the party were able to hide about them when they escaped from Goa, and yet wandered and voyaged at large and alone about India and the Indian seas for the space of four full years.

Certainly Osborne and Staper chose their dark horse shrewdly. Not less well chosen, one supposes, were

Leedes the jeweller and Story the painter. European, though not English, craftsmen were known and welcome enough at the Mughal court and a jeweller, especially, was no bad thin end of this slender adventured wedge. Our precursor of Tavernier and Thévenot had the wit and skill to find a comfortable nook for himself in Akbar's household, and this was the sort of man to be a useful ally. Story also, who did well for himself with singular neatness at Goa. Other things apart, there is no doubting the courage of these two.

The plan of action concerted by the band was quite simple in outline. Eldred, halted between Basra and Baghdad, was to be, as it were, the shaft of the spear, the other four its head thrusting forward into India. Though shaft and head came apart the thrust did in fact go home.

All that happened is too plainly told to need comment here, but a few general aspects may be usefully touched upon.

Apart from the uncertain figures of the Middle Ages, three of these four were the first Englishmen to penetrate fairly to the heart of India; the fourth, Fitch, went beyond to Burma where no Englishman at all had ever been. These were great feats in themselves; the greater when it is considered that they were escaped prisoners; that their captors, the

Portuguese, held every European settlement in India, and that the interior of the country was almost wholly unknown. How the three travelled or managed to exist we cannot tell. Fitch did not think it worth while to give any details and neither of the others has left any known record. We can be sure they wore native costume, both because this was long the custom of early Europeans in India, where notice always contemptuous and frequently hostile had to be avoided as much as possible, and because the hue and cry was after them. We know from the massacre of Amboina how the later Dutch treated interlopers, and the Portuguese were no more merciful. By themselves they might in time have called off the hunt, but they had Philip of Spain to spur them to it afresh. There are extant four letters of his to the Viceroy, Duarte de Menezes, earnestly enquiring for these pestilent Englishmen; they are dated February 25th, 1585; February 13th, 1587; February 2nd, 1589; and January 12th, 1591. Philip had the tenacity proper to a slow mind. By the time the first can have reached Goa the birds were already some time flown; the second would find Fitch somewhere in Burma; the third may have reached Goa only two or three months before he came there for the second time—an apt encounter. Perhaps he smelt something of a stir; at any rate he only stayed three days.

By the time the fourth was written he was out of India ; by the time it arrived, safely recreating himself at home. It was Philip's way to be a day too late for the fair.

Perhaps too much has been made of the daring of Fitch's return to Goa. Disguised, sun-burnt, travel-changed, he would not be easily recognised. Anyhow, he was used to walking serenely into traps and out again ; the Portuguese towns of Bengal, Pegu, Malacca, Ceylon ; the Malabar ports and every ship he sailed on would provide them in plenty almost as lightly set. No doubt he had an audacity.

High audacity, of course, is the key-note of the whole adventure from its inception, but we forget it because what we are told we are told in so calm a tone. We become conscious of it, perhaps, at the swift plunge into the dark of the escape from Goa, and then partly because the effect is heightened by the fine comedy played before Linschoten. That grave Dutchman's acceptance of all the tears and fears so ingenuously displayed before him ; the venomous cynicism of his attitude to the Jesuits (he remembered Alva), and his hurt bewilderment at the sudden impish end of the play, compose a picture of the richest latent humour. One wonders with relish, too, what sort of information Story gave him and whether he gave it with his tongue in his cheek.

It is a delight to note how many latent significances of all sorts Hakluyt—the perfect editor—allows to show themselves. He permits a moderate piety (it was, beside, the custom of the age), even, in the case of Stevens and Frey Peter, a hint of preaching and a trifle more piety ; a churchman himself he knew what was becoming in a churchman. All else not strictly relevant to the story he cuts out with the most remorseless knife in the history of letters, and yet always manages to leave the grain of leaven here and there which lightens the whole mass. Such grains, among plenty, are Eldred's " bribing dogs ", Fitch's comments on Hindu ritual, his shorthand opinion of the Brahmans and his holy man of Patna, while our chief three somehow manage to etch their own characters with amazing sureness ; it is a matter, perhaps, of leaving out the right lines. We have Eldred very aware and canny ; a shade of toughness about his heart and of coolness in his emotions generally ; quite staunch, but economical in lament when a comrade went out of action. Fitch has been already glanced at ; one may remark in him, further, a curious gaiety or sunniness—it is difficult to find the right word. A touch of the indomitable boy, perhaps. Apart from the sheer insolent courage that could set off alone on the journey to Lahore and so home through Persia, Newbery impresses one chiefly by a hint of the bee in his nature. Anxiously preoccupied with his affairs ; serious, careful and inclined to be fretty about their details ; very ready to be extremely irritable if deflected from his pursuit of them, or virulently furious at the mere name of Michael Stropene, he does suggest the bee—and, again, the bee's courage. A likeable man, but difficult to live with at times we may dare to suppose.

Touching Newbery, there is a small mystery about him which had best be dealt with here. It has always been assumed, and, I believe, rightly, that he was never heard of again after he left for Lahore. We are directly told (by Fitch himself and by Eldred) of Fitch's return, but neither says a word about the return of Newbery. We hear in other ways—to be next mentioned—of the returned Fitch, but in no way whatever do we hear anything of a returned Newbery. The inference is plain that he never did return, but there is one puzzling fact. In his own account, given in Purchas, of his former journey to Hormuz and Persia (1580 to 1582), he uses these words : " And in very deed, in my last voyage into these parts, in the year 1583, this Michael Stropene betrayed me and my company to the Governor of Ormus ". The question is obvious—when was that written ? Naturally, there were plenty of opportunities for the writing at any time after the imprisonment at Hormuz ; during the period of freedom at Goa, for instance, or their stay at Agra and Fatehpur Sikri, or even some interval in between, and there are many other possibilities ; but in any of these cases there is the further question—how was the bulky manuscript of which these words formed part sent home ? It might have been done through the friendly Stevens, or Fitch might have carried the pages with him all those years and miles ; either way is possible, neither is likely. The Portuguese had a fairly searching censorship ; Fitch certainly had to travel light, and in either or any conceivable case it is strange to the point of incredibility that no one should so much as mention the business. Again, that phrase " in my last voyage into these parts ". By the feel of it either that was written after some safe return or Newbery was capable of a detachment perfectly inhuman. We owe Purchas much, but he was a most disarranged kind of editor and it is entirely like him to have garbled something or omitted what would have illuminated the whole mystery ; as it is, we are left wondering whether Newbery did in fact get home, or if not how in the world his manuscript did so. There is nothing against his having returned except the fact that no one says another word about him, alive or dead, and the additional fact that there are very good reasons for expecting that word if he were alive.

Those reasons appear in what is the sequel of the whole great adventure.

Fitch returned in 1591 to a strange England freed, by the defeat of the Armada, from a multitude of hesitations and fears and kindling with new ardours. He brought great news himself to increase the flame and found old friends very eager to hear it. That it was heard and acted upon we can rightly infer from the fact that in 1592 Elizabeth granted a Charter for the second Levant Company in which were named, among others, as governors or members for twelve years, Sir Edward Osborne and Masters Hareborne, Staper, Power (the "Leonard Poore" of our text), Shales, Eldred and Fitch. Newbery would certainly have shared in these firstfruits of the voyage he had piloted until his disappearance he was too valuable to be left out.

Then in 1599 the full fruits began to come. The Levant Company was not enough, for the overland route was too difficult ; England had now the freedom of all the seas and could send her ships where she chose ; Fitch's story, then just published by Hakluyt, was stirring all London, and so at length the merchants resolved to do decisively what they had many times failed in—get leave from Elizabeth to form a company for trading with India direct by sea. What with captured documents ; oddments of experience ; Hakluyt's accumulating store of facts, and the 1598 translation of Linschoten's great book, enough was known to make the navigation commercially possible, and there was Fitch to tell them all he knew about the land.

So on 24th September, 1599, eighty merchants met at Founders' Hall to debate and resolve ; Fitch and Eldred were there to inform and advise. A year's hard work and Court intrigue, and there was another meeting at Founders' Hall on the 23rd September, 1600, and another on the 2nd October ; at the latter, we read in the Court Minutes of the yet unborn Company how it was "Ordered that . . . Master Eldred and Master Fitch shall in the meeting to-morrow morning confer of the merchandise fit to be provided for the first voyage ". Things were moving now, and on the 31st December, 1600, Elizabeth granted their first Charter to the East India Company. That spear-thrust had gone home.

The later story of the Company is part of general history and need not be told here. But an entry in its Court Minutes concerns us. It is dated the 31st December, 1606, and reads : " Letters to be obtained from King James to the King of Cambaya, governors of Aden, etc. . . . their titles to be enquired of Ralph Fitch ". That is the last ever heard of him. One hopes life used him well.

It will be seen that Newbery appears in none of this, as he was certain to appear if alive and in England. It is certain, too, that if he had returned Hakluyt would have extracted an account of the Indian journey from him. So we must suppose he never did return, which leaves the problem of his fate the problem stated still.

It is so, indeed, with all our five chief travellers, excepting Eldred. Of him we know that he was born in 1552 at New Buckenham in Norfolk, became wealthy and built a fine house for himself—nicknamed " Nutmeg Hall "—at Great Saxham in Suffolk, died there and was buried in the church, where his monument is, on the 8th December, 1632, and much else besides. There is Newbery's account in Purchas of his earlier travels, but beyond this and what is given here and in the text, nothing ; with Fitch, Leedes and Story it is the same. It would be well if some one some day could find out more about them, for they did great work.

Before we leave them all it may as well be said that Eldred and Fitch need lose no credit because here and there they take bits from the Italian, Cesare Federici—Englished in Hakluyt as " Caesar Frederick ". It was the custom of the age and one certain to be followed by unwilling writers goaded to their job by the relentless Hakluyt, while at least the fabulous elements in the earlier writers tended to diminish with every successive repetition. An instance is Fitch's estimate of the armed strength of Pegu, which is much more sober than that of Federici—even than that of Frey Peter who wrote only a couple of years or so earlier than Fitch.

A word as to the inclusion of Frey Peter's letter. In the first place, it was a document hoarded and pored over by Hakluyt and the founders of the Company, as throwing more light on this wonderful new Kingdom of Pegu that Fitch had stumbled upon : in the second, it is impressive with foreboding of that storm soon to wreck the Spanish dominion in the East, and with that strange Prophecy of the Dragon.

Stevens' letter explains itself. It was another of Hakluyt's treasured guiding-documents and as such entrusted by him to our travellers ; and it fittingly completes the picture of that band who were first of the modern English to reach India, though they journeyed in their several times and by their several roads.

The First Englishmen in India

A letter written from Goa, the principal City of all the East Indies, by one Thomas Stevens[1]*, an Englishman, and sent to his father Master Thomas Stevens, Anno* 1579.

AFTER most humble commendations these shall be to crave your daily blessing, with like commendations unto my mother, and withal to certify[2] you of my being[3]; according to your will and my duty.

I wrote unto you taking my journey from Italy to Portugal, which letters I think are come to your hands; so that, presuming thereupon, I think I have the less need at this time to tell you the cause of my departing, which nevertheless in one word I may conclude[4], if I do but name Obedience[5].

I came to Lisbon toward the end of March, eight days before the departure of the ships; so late, that if they had not been stayed about some weighty matters they had been long gone before our coming; insomuch that there were others ordained[6] to go in our places, that the King's provision and ours also might not be in vain. Nevertheless our sudden coming took place, and the 4th of April five ships departed for Goa; wherein, besides shipmen and soldiers, there were a great number of children, which in the seas bear out better than men ; and no marvel, when that many women also pass very well.

The setting forth from the port, I need not to tell how solemn it is, with trumpets and shooting of ordnance. You may easily imagine it, considering that they go in the manner of war.

The 10th of the foresaid month we came to the sight of Porto Santo, near unto Madera[1], where an English ship set upon ours (which was then also alone) with a few shots which did no harm. But after that our ship had laid out her greatest ordnance they straight departed as they came.

The English ship was very fair and great, which I was sorry to see so ill-occupied, for she went roving about, so that we saw her again at the Canarian Isles, unto the which we came the 13th of the said month. And good leisure we had to wonder at the high mountain of the Island Tenerif, for we wandered between that and Great Canaria four days by reason of contrary winds. And, briefly, such evil weather we had until the 14th of May that they despaired to compass the Cape of Good Hope that year.

Nevertheless, taking our voyage between Guinea and the Islands of Capo Verde, without seeing of any land at all, we arrived at length unto the coast of Guinea which the Portugals so call ; chiefly that part

VIEW OF LISBON ABOUT 1570

[facing p. 20

of the Burning Zone which is from the sixth degree unto the Equinoctial[1].

In which parts they suffered so many inconveniences of heats and lack of winds that they think themselves happy when they have passed it. For sometimes the ship standeth there, almost, by the space of many days; sometime she goeth, but in such order that it were almost as good to stand still. And the greatest part of this coast not clear, but thick and cloudy; full of thunder and lightning, and rain so unwholesome that if the water stand a little while all is full of worms, and falling on the meat which is hanged up it maketh it straight full of worms[2].

Along all that coast we oftentimes saw a thing swimming upon the water like a cock's comb, which they call a Ship of Guinea, but the colour much fairer. Which comb standeth upon a thing almost like the swimmer of a fish in colour and bigness, and beareth underneath in the water strings which save it from turning over. This thing is so poisonous that a man cannot touch it without great peril[3].

In this coast—that is to say, from the sixth degree unto the Equinoctial—we spent no less than thirty days; partly with contrary winds, partly with calm.

The 30th of May we passed the Equinoctial with contentation, directing our course as well as we could to pass the Promontory[4]. But in all that gulf, and in all the way beside, we found so often calms that the expertest mariners wondered at it. And in places where are always wont to be most horrible tempests we found most quiet calms ; which was very troublesome to those ships which be the greatest of all other and cannot go without good winds. Insomuch that when it is tempest almost intolerable for other ships and maketh them maine all their sails, these hoise[1] up and sail excellent well, unless the waters be too, too furious, which seldom happened in our navigation.

You shall understand that being passed the Line they cannot straightway go the next[2] way to the Promontory, but according to the wind they draw always as near South as they can, to put themselves in the latitude of the Point[3]—which is 35 degrees and an half—and then they take their course towards the East and so compass the Point. But the wind served us so, that at 33 degrees we did direct our course toward the Point or Promontory of Good Hope.

You know that it is hard to sail from East to West or contrary, because there is no fixed point in all the sky whereby they may direct their course ; wherefore I shall tell you what helps God provided for these men. There is not a fowl that appeareth, or sign in the air or in the sea, which they have not written which have made the voyages heretofore. Wherefore, partly by their own experience, and pondering, withal, what space the ship was able to make with such a wind and such direction, and partly by the experience of others, whose books and navigations they have, they guess whereabouts they be, touching degrees of longitude, for of latitude they be always sure[1].

But the greatest and best industry of all is to mark the variation of the needle, or compass ; which in the meridian of the Island of St. Michael (which is one of the Azores in the latitude of Lisbon) is just North[2], and thence swarveth[3] towards the East so much that betwixt the Meridian aforesaid and the Point of Africa[4] it carrieth three or four quarters of thirty-two[5]. And again, in the Point of Africa, a little beyond the point that is called Cape das Agulias (in English, The Needles), it returneth again unto the North ; and that place passed, it swarveth again toward the West, as it did before proportionally[6].

As touching our first signs, the nearer we came to the people[7] of Africa the more strange kinds of fowls appeared ; insomuch that when we came within no less than thirty leagues (almost an hundred miles), and six hundred miles, as we thought, from any Island, as good as three thousand fowls of sundry kinds followed our ship, some of them so great that their wings, being opened, from one point to the other contained seven spans[8], as the Mariners said.

A marvellous thing to see how God provided ; so that in so wide a sea these fowls are all fat and nothing wanteth them[1].

The Portugals have named them all according to some propriety[2] which they have. Some they call Rushtails, because their tails be not proportionable to their bodies but long and small like a rush ; some Forked Tails, because they be very broad and forked ; some Velvet Sleeves, because they have wings of the colour of velvet and bow them as a man boweth his elbow[3]. This bird is always welcome, for he appeareth nearest the Cape.

I should never make an end if I should tell all particulars, but it shall suffice briefly to touch a few ; which yet shall be sufficient, if you mark them, to give occasion to glorify Almighty God in His wonderful works and such variety in His creatures.

And to speak somewhat of fishes : in all places of calm, especially in the Burning Zone near the Line (for without we never saw any), there waited on our ship fishes as long as a man, which they call Tuberones[4]. They come to eat such things as from the ship fall into the sea, not refusing men themselves if they light upon them ; and if they find any meat tied in the sea they take it for theirs. These have waiting on them six or seven small fishes (which never depart) with gardes[5] blue and green round about their bodies, like comely serving-men ; and they go two or three before him and some on every side[1]. Moreover they have other fishes which cleave always unto their body and seem to take such superfluities as grow about them ; and they are said to enter into their bodies also to purge them if they need[2]. The Mariners in time past have eaten of them[3], but since they have seen them eat men their stomachs abhor them. Nevertheless, they draw them up with great hooks, and kill of them as many as they can, thinking that they have made a great revenge.

There is another kind of fish as big, almost, as a herring, which hath wings and flieth, and they are together in great number. These have two enemies, the one in the sea, the other in the air. In the sea the fish which is called Albocore[4], as big as a Salmon, followeth them with great swiftness to take them. This poor fish, not being able to swim fast (for he hath no fins but swimmeth with moving of his tail), shutting his wings, lifteth himself above the water and flieth not very high. The Albocore seeing that, although he have no wings yet he giveth a great leap out of the water, and sometimes catcheth him ; or else he keepeth himself under the water, going that way on as fast as he flieth, and when the fish—being weary of the air or thinking himself out of danger—returneth into the water the Albocore meeteth with him, but sometimes his other enemy, the Sea-Crow, catcheth him before he falleth[1].

With these and like sights, but always making our supplications to God for good weather and salvation of the ship, we came at length unto the Point, so famous and feared of all men[2] (but we found there no tempeſt, only great waves), where our Pilot was a little overseen[3]. For whereas commonly all other never come within sight of land, but seeing signs ordinary and finding bottom go their way sure and safe, he—thinking himself to have wind at will—shot so nigh the land that the wind turning into the South and the waves being exceeding great rolled us so near the land that the ship ſtood in less than fourteen fathoms of water, no more than six miles from the Cape which is called Das Agulias. And there we ſtood as utterly caſt away; for under us were rocks of main[4] ſtone so sharp and cutting that no anchor could hold the ship, the shore so evil that nothing could take land, and the land itself so full of Tigers[5] and people that are savage and killers of all ſtrangers that we had no hope of life nor comfort, but only in God and a good conscience. Notwithſtanding, after we had loſt anchors, hoising up the sails for to get the ship a coaſt in some safer place or when it should please God, it pleased His mercy suddenly, where no man looked for help, to fill our sails with wind from the land. And so we escaped, thanks be to God.

And the day following, being in the place where they are always wont to catch fish, we also fell a-fishing; and so many they took that they served all the ship for that day and part of the next. And one of them pulled up a coral of great bigness and price; for there they say (as we saw by experience) that the corals do grow in the manner of stalks upon the rocks in the bottom and wax hard and red. The day of peril was the 29th of July.

And you shall understand that, the Cape passed, there be two ways to India; one within the Isle of St. Laurence[1], which they take willingly because they refresh themselves at Mosambique a fortnight or a month, not without great need, and thence in a month more land in Goa.

The other is without the Isle of St. Laurence, which they take when they set forth so late and come so late to the Point that they have no time to take the foresaid Mosambique; and then they go heavily[2], because in this way they take no port. And by reason of the long navigation and want of food and water they fall into sundry diseases; their gums wax great and swell and they are fain to cut them away, their legs swell and all the body becometh sore, and so benumbed that they cannot stir hand nor foot, and so they die for weakness. Others fall into fluxes and agues and die thereby[1].

And this way it was our chance to make, yet though we had more than one hundred and fifty sick there died not past seven and twenty ; which loss they esteemed not much in respect of other times[2]. Though some of ours[3] were diseased in this sort, yet, thanks be to God, I had my health all the way, contrary to the expectation of many. God send me my health so well in the land, if it may be to His honour and service.

This way is full of privy[4] rocks and quicksands, so that sometimes we durst not sail by night ; but by the providence of God we saw nothing nor never found bottom until we came to the coast of India.

When we had passed again the Line and were come to the third degree or somewhat more we saw crabs swimming on the water that were red as though they had been sodden[5] ; but this was no sign of land. After, about the eleventh degree, the space of many days more than ten thousand fishes, by estimation, followed round about our ship ; whereof we caught so many that for fifteen days we did eat nothing else, and they served our turn very well. For at this time we had neither meat nor almost anything else to eat, our navigation growing so long that it drew near to seven months, whereas commonly they go it in five. I mean when they sail the inner way. But these fishes were not sign of land, but rather of deep sea.

At length we took a couple of birds, which were a kind of Hawks, whereof they joyed much, thinking that they had been of India, but indeed they were of Arabia, as we found afterward. And we that thought we had been near India were in the same latitude near Zocotoro[1], an Isle in the mouth of the Red Sea. But there God sent us great winds from the North-east or North-north-east, whereupon unwillingly they bare up toward the East ; and thus we went ten days without seeing sign of land, whereby they perceived their error.

For they had directed their course before always North-east, coveting to multiply degrees of latitude[2] ; but partly the difference of the Needle, and, most of all, the running seas (which at that time ran North-west), had drawn us to this other danger[3] had not God sent us this wind, which at length waxed larger and restored us to our right course.

These running seas be so perilous that they deceive the most part of the governors[4] ; and some be so little curious, contenting themselves with ordinary experience, that they care not to seek out any means to know when they swarve, neither by the compass nor by any other trial.

The first sign of land were certain fowls which they knew to be of India ; the second, boughs of palms and sedges ; the third, snakes swimming on the water, and a substance which they call by the name of a coin of money, as broad and as round as a groat, wonderfully printed and stamped of nature ; like unto some coin[1]. And these two last signs be so certain that the next day after, if the wind serve, they see land. Which we did, to our great joy, when all our water (for you know they make no beer in those parts[2]) and victuals began to fail us.

And to Goa we came the 24th day of October, there being received with passing great charity.

The people be tawny, but not disfigured in their lips and noses, as the Moors and Cafres[3] of Ethiopia. They that be not of reputation—or, at least, the most part—go naked, saving an apron of a span long and as much in breadth before them, and a lace[4] two fingers broad before them girded about with a string, and no more. And thus they think themselves as well as we with all our trimming.

Of the fruits and trees that be here I cannot now speak, for I should make another letter as long as this. For hitherto I have not seen a tree here whose like I have seen in Europe, the vine excepted, which, nevertheless, here is to no purpose, so that all the wines are brought out of Portugal.

The drink of this country is good water, or wine of the Palm tree[5] or of a fruit called Cocos[6].

And this shall suffice for this time. If God send me my health I shall have opportunity to write to you once again. Now the length of my letter compelleth me to take my leave ; and thus I wish your most prosperous health.

From Goa, the 10th of November 1579.

Your loving son Thomas Stevens.

Here is set a Letter[1] *written by the Queen's Majesty to Zelabdim Echebar,*[2] *King of Cambaia,*[3] *and sent by John Newbery. In February, Anno* 1583.

Elizabeth by the grace of God etc. To the most invincible and most mighty Prince, Lord Zelabdim Echebar, King of Cambaia ; Invincible Emperor, etc.

The great affection[4] which our Subjects have to visit the most distant places of the world (not without good will and intention to introduce the trade of merchandise of all nations whatsoever they can ; by which means the mutual and friendly traffic of merchandise on both sides may come), is the cause that the bearer of this letter, John Newbery, jointly with those that be in his company, with a courteous and honest boldness do repair to the borders and countries of your Empire. We doubt not but that your Imperial Majesty, through your royal grace, will favourably and friendly accept him. And that you would do it the rather for our sake, to make us greatly beholding[1] to your Majesty, we should more earnestly and with more words require it if we did think it needful. But by the singular report that is of your Imperial Majesty's humanity in these uttermost parts of the world we are greatly eased of that burden, and therefore we use the fewer and less words. Only we request that because they are our subjects they may be honestly entreated and received, and that in respect of the hard journey which they have undertaken to places so far distant it would please your Majesty with some liberty and security of voyage to gratify it[2], with such privileges as to you shall seem good. Which courtesy if your Imperial Majesty shall to our subjects at our requests perform, We, according to our Royal Honour, will recompense the same with as many deserts as we can.

And herewith we bid your Imperial Majesty to farewell.

And here a Letter written by her Majesty to the King of China, in February, 1583.

Elizabeth, by the grace of God, Queen of England, etc. Most Imperial and invincible Prince.

Our honest subject, John Newbery, the bringer hereof, who, with our favour, hath taken in hand the voyage which now he pursueth to the parts and countries of your Empire, not trusting upon any other ground than upon the favour of your Imperial clemency and humanity, is moved to undertake a thing of so much difficulty, being persuaded that, he having entered into so many perils, your Majesty will not dislike the same, especially if it may appear that it be not damageable unto your Royal Majesty, and that to your people it will bring some profit. Of both which things he not doubting, with more willing mind hath prepared himself for his predestinated voyage—unto us well liked of.

For by this means we perceive that the profit which, by the mutual trade on both sides, all the princes our neighbours in the West do receive, your Imperial Majesty and those that be subject under your dominion to their great joy and benefit, shall have the same ; which consisteth in the transporting outward of such things whereof we have plenty and in bringing in such things as we stand in need of. It cannot otherwise be (but that), seeing we are born and made to have need one of another, and that we are bound to aid one another, but that[1] your Imperial Majesty will well like of it, and by your subjects with like endeavour will be accepted.

For the increase whereof, if your Imperial Majesty shall add the security of passage, with other privileges most necessary to use the trade with your men, your Majesty shall do that which belongeth to a most honourable and liberal Prince, and deserve so much of us as by no continuance or length of time shall be forgotten.

Which request of ours We do most instantly[1] desire to be taken in good part of your Majesty ; and so great a benefit towards us and our men we shall endeavour by diligence to requite when time shall serve thereunto.

The God Almighty long preserve your Imperial Majesty.

Here beginneth the Voyage of Master John Eldred to Tripolis[2] in Syria by sea, and from thence by land and river to Babylon[3] and Balsara[4].

I departed out of London in the ship called the *Tiger*, in the company of Master John Newbery, Master Ralph Fitch and six or seven other honest merchants, upon Shrove Monday[5], 1583, and arrived in Tripolis of Syria the 1st day of May next ensuing[6]. At our landing we went a-maying upon St. George's Island, a place where Christians dying aboard the ships are wont to be buried.

In this city our English merchants have a Consul, and our nation abide together in one house with him, called *Fondeghi Ingles*[1], builded of ſtone, square in manner like a Cloiſter ; and every man hath his several[2] chamber, as it is the use there of all other Chriſtians of several nations.

This town ſtandeth under a part of the mountain of Libanus[3], two English miles diſtant from the port ; on the side of which port, trending in form of an half Moon, ſtand five blockhouses or small forts[4], wherein is some very good artillery, and the forts are kept with about an hundred Janissaries[5].

Right before this town from the seaward is a bank of moving sand, which gathereth and increaseth with the Weſtern winds in such sort that, according to an old prophecy among them, this bank is like to swallow up and overwhelm the town, for every year it increaseth and eateth up many gardens, although they use all policy to diminish the same and to make it firm ground[6].

The city is about the bigness of Briſtow[7] and walled about, though the walls be of no great force. The chief ſtrength of the place is in a Citadel, which ſtandeth on the South side, within the walls, and overlooketh the whole town and is ſtrongly kept with two hundred Janissaries and good artillery. A river passeth through the midſt of the city, wherewith they water their gardens and mulberry trees, on which there grow abundance of silk-worms wherewith they make great quantity of very white silk, which is the chiefest natural commodity to be found in and about this place.

This road[1] is more frequented with Christian merchants, to wit, Venetians, Genoese, Florentines, Marseillians, Sicilians, Raguseans, and lately with Englishmen, than any other port of the Turk's dominions.

From Tripolis I departed the 14th of May with a caravan, passing three days over the ridge of Mount Libanus, at the end whereof we arrived in a city called Hammah[2], which standeth on a goodly plain replenished with corn and cotton-wool[3]. On these mountains which we passed grow great quantity of gall trees, which are somewhat like our oaks but lesser and more crooked ; on the best tree a man shall not find above a pound of galls[4]. This town of Hammah is fallen and falleth more and more to decay, and at this day there is scarce one half of the wall standing, which hath been very strong and fair. But because it cost many men's lives to win it the Turk will not have it repaired, and hath written in the Arabian tongue over the Castle gate, which standeth in the midst of the town, these words : "Cursed be the father and the son that shall lay their hands to the repairing hereof"[5]. Refreshing ourselves one day here, we passed forward with camels

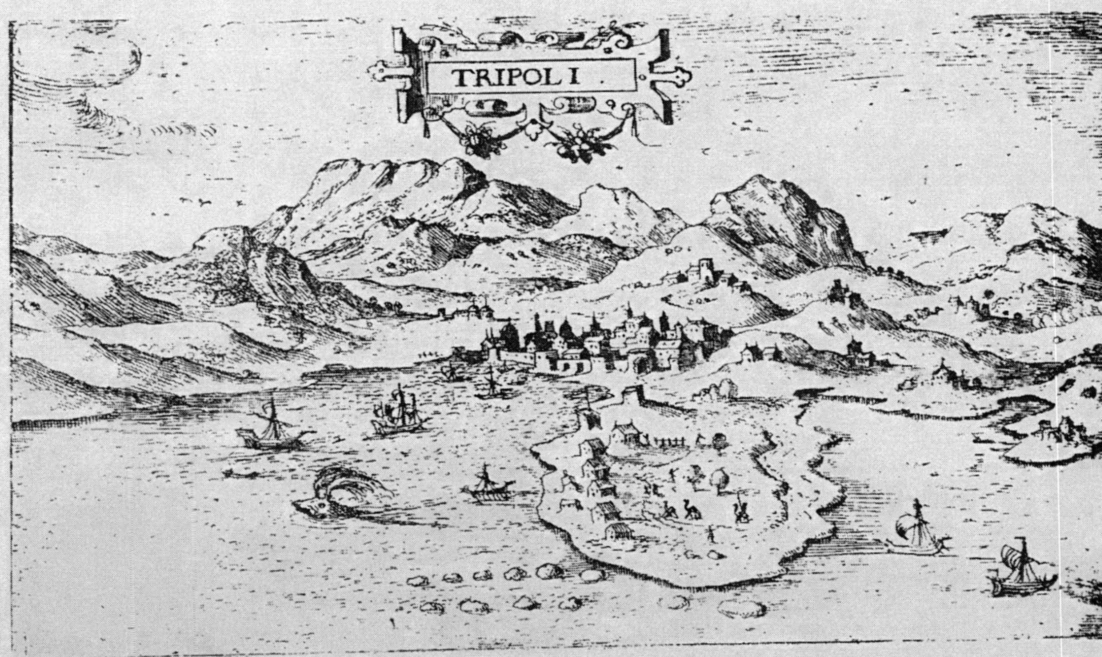

VIEW OF TRIPOLI ABOUT 1610

[facing p. 36

three days more until we came to Aleppo, where we arrived the 21st of May.

This is the greatest place of traffic for a dry town[1] that is in all those parts, for hither resort Jews, Tartarians, Persians, Armenians, Egyptians, Indians, and many sorts of Christians, and enjoy freedom of their consciences and bring thither many kinds of rich merchandises. In the midst of this town, also, standeth a goodly Castle raised on high[2], with a garrison of four or five hundred Janissaries. Within four miles round about are goodly gardens and vineyards, and trees which bear goodly fruit near unto the river's side, which is but small[3]. The walls are about three English miles in compass, but the suburbs are almost as much more. The town is greatly peopled.

Here is set a Letter of Master John Newbery, written from Aleppo to Master Richard Hakluyt[4] of Oxford, the 28th of May, Anno 1583.

Right well beloved and my assured good friend, I heartily commend me unto you hoping of your good health, etc.

After we set sail from Gravesend, which was the 13th day of February last, we remained upon our coast until the 11th day of March, and that day we set sail from Falmouth, and never anchored till we arrived in the road of Tripolis in Syria, which was the last day of April last past; where we stayed fourteen days. And the 20th[1] of this present we came hither to Aleppo, and, with God's help, within five or six days go from hence towards the Indies.

Since my coming to Tripoli I have made very earnest enquiry, both there and here, for the book of Cosmography of Abilfada Ismael[2], but by no means can hear of it. Some say that possibly it may be had in Persia, but, notwithstanding, I will not fail to make enquiry for it, both in Babylon and in Balsara, and if I can find it in any of these places I will send it you from thence.

The letter which you delivered me for to copy out (that came from Master Thomas Stevens in Goa[3]) as also the note you gave me of Francis Fernandez the Portugal[4], I brought thence with me among other writings unawares; the which I have sent you here enclosed.

Here is great preparation for the wars in Persia and from hence is gone the Bassa[5] of a town called Rahemet[6], and shortly after goeth the Bassa of Tripolis; and the Bassa of Damasco[7], but they have not all with them above six thousand men from hence; and they go to a town called Asmerome, which is three days' journey from Trapezunde[1], where they shall meet with divers captains and soldiers that come from Constantinople and other places thereabout, which go all together into Persia.

This year many men go into the wars, and so hath there every year since the beginning thereof, which is eight years or thereabouts[2], but very few of them return again. Notwithstanding, they get of the Persians and make castles and holds in their country.

I pray you make my hearty commendations to Master Peter Guillame and Master Philip Jones, and to Master Walter Warner and to all the rest of our friends. Master Fitch hath him heartily commended unto you.

And so I commit you to the tuition[3] of the Almighty Who bless and keep you and send us a joyful meeting.

From Aleppo, the 28th of May, 1583.

Your loving friend to commend in all that I may,

John Newbery.

And here another Letter of the said Master Newbery; written to Master Leonard Poore of London, from Aleppo, the 29th May, 1583.

Right well beloved,

My very hearty commendations unto you, and the rest of my friends remembered.

My last I sent you was the 25th of February last, from Deal out of the Downs. After which time, with contrary winds, we remained upon our own coast until the 11th day of March; and then we set sail from Falmouth, and the thirteenth day the wind came contrary with a very great storm which continued eight days, and in this great storm we had some of our goods wet but God be thanked, no great hurt done.

After which time we sailed with a fair wind within the Straits[1], and so remained at sea and anchored at no place until our coming into the road of Tripolis in Syria, which was the last day of April. This was a very good passage; God make us thankful for it.

The 14th day of this present we came from Tripolis and the 20th day arrived here in Aleppo, and, with the help of God, to-morrow or next day we begin our voyage towards Babylon and Balsara and so into India.

Our friend Master Barret[2] hath him commended to you; who hath sent you, in the *Emanuel*, a ball[3] of Nutmegs for the small trifles you sent him, which I hope long since you have received. Also he hath by his letter certified you in what order[4] he sold those things, whereof I can say nothing, because I have not seen the account thereof neither have demanded it; for ever since our coming hither he hath been still busy about the despatch of the ship and our voyage[1], and I likewise in buying of things here to carry to Balsara and the Indies.

We have bought in currall[2] for twelve hundred and odd ducats, and amber for four hundred ducats, and some soap and broken glass[3] with all other small trifles ; all which things I hope will serve very well for those places that we shall go unto.

All the reſt of the account of the bark *Reynolds* was sent home in the *Emanuel*, which was 3,600 ducats[4], which is £200 more than it was rated[5]. For Maſter Staper rated it but £1,100 and it is £1,300, so that our part is £200, besides such profit as it shall please God to send thereof ; wherefore you shall do very well to speak to Maſter Staper for the account.

And if you would content yourself to travel for three or four years I would wish you to come hither or go to Cairo, if any go thither. For we doubt not, if you had remained there but three or four months, you would like so well of the place that I think you would not desire to return again in three or four years.

And if it should be my chance to remain in any place out of England I would choose this before all other that I know. My reason is, the place is healthful and pleasant and the gains very good, and no doubt the profit will be hereafter better, things being used in good order; for there should come in every ship the fourth part of her Cargason[1] in money, which would help to put away our commodities at a very good price. Also, to have two very good ships to come together would do very well; for in so doing the danger[2] of the voyage might be accounted as little as from London to Antwerp.

Master Giles Porter and Master Edmund Porter went from Tripolis in a small bark to Jaffa, the same day that we came from thence, which was the 14th day of this present; so that no doubt but long since they are in Jerusalem. God send them and us safe return.

At this instant I have received the account of Master Barret and the rest of the rings, with two and twenty ducats, two medines[3], in ready money; so there is nothing remaining in his hands but a few books. And with Thomas Bostocke I left certain small trifles, which I pray you demand.

And so once again, with my hearty commendations, I commit you to the tuition of the Almighty, Who always preserve us.

From Aleppo, the 29th of May, 1583.

Yours assured,

John Newbery.

Here is continued the Relation of Master John Eldred:

We departed from thence with our camels the last of May, with Master John Newbery and his company, and came to Birrah[1] in three days, being a small town situated upon the river Euphrates where it beginneth first to take his name, being here gathered into one channel whereas before it cometh down in manifold branches, and therefore is called by the people of the country by a name which signifieth "a thousand heads"[2]. Here is plenty of victuals, whereof we all furnished ourselves for a long journey down the aforesaid river, and according to the manner of those that travel down by water we prepared a small bark for the conveyance of ourselves and of our goods. These boats are flat bottomed[3], because the river is shallow in many places, and when men travel in the months of July, August and September, the water being then at the lowest, they are constrained to carry with them a spare boat or two, to lighten their own boats if they chance to fall on the sholds[4].

We were eight and twenty days upon the water between Birrah and Felugia[5], where we disembarked ourselves and our goods. Every night after the Sun setteth we tie our bark to a stake, go on land to gather sticks, and set on our pot with rice or bruised wheat, and, having supped, the merchants lie aboard the bark and the mariners upon the shore's side, as near as they can unto the same. In many places upon the river's side we met with troops of Arabians, of whom we bought milk, butter, eggs and lambs and gave them in barter (for they care not for money) glasses, combs, coral, amber, to hang about their arms and necks, and for churned milk we gave them bread and pomegranate peels, wherewith they use[1] to tan their goats' skins which they churn withal[2]. Their hair, apparel and colour are altogether like to those vagabond Egyptians[3] which heretofore have gone about in England. Their women all without exception wear a great round ring in one of their nostrils, of gold, silver or iron according to their ability, and about their arms and smalls of their legs they have hoops of gold, silver or iron. All of them, as well women and children as men, are very great swimmers, and, oftentimes, swimming they brought us milk to our bark in vessels upon their heads. These people are very thievish, which I proved to my cost, for they stole a casket of mine, with things of good value in the same, from under my man's head as he was asleep ; and therefore travellers keep good watch as they pass down the river. Euphrates at Birrah is about the breadth of the Thames at Lambeth, and in some places narrower, in some broader ; it runneth very swiftly, almost as fast as the river of

Trent. It hath divers sorts of fish in it, but all are scaled, some as big as salmons, like barbels.

We landed at Felugia the 28th of June, where we made our abode seven days, for lack of camels to carry our goods to Babylon. The heat at that time of the year is such in those parts that men are loath to let out their camels to travel. This Felugia is a village of some hundred houses, and a place appointed for the discharging of such goods as come down the river ; the inhabitants are Arabians. Not finding camels here, we were constrained to unlade our goods, and hired an hundred asses to carry our English merchandises only to New Babylon over a short desert[1], in crossing whereof we spent eighteen hours, travelling by night and part of the morning to avoid the great heat.

In this place which we crossed over stood the old mighty city of Babylon[2], many old ruins whereof are easily to be seen by daylight, which I, John Eldred, have often beheld at my good leisure, having made three voyages between the new city of Babylon and Aleppo, over this desert. Here also are yet standing the ruins of the old tower of Babel, which, being upon a plain ground, seemeth afar off very great, but the nearer you come to it the lesser and lesser it appeareth ; sundry times I have gone thither to see it, and found the remnants yet standing above a quarter of a mile in compass and almost as high as the stone-work of Paul's steeple in London[1], but it showeth much bigger. The bricks remaining in this most ancient monument be half a yard thick and three quarters of a yard long, being dried in the Sun only, and between every course of bricks there lieth a course of mats made of canes, which remain sound and not perished, as though they had been laid within one year[2].

The city of New Babylon joineth upon the aforesaid small desert where the old city was, and the river of Tigris runneth close unto the wall ; and they may, if they will, open a sluice and let the waters of the same run round about the town. It is above two English miles in compass, and the inhabitants generally speak three languages, to wit, the Persian, Arabian and Turkish tongues. The people are of the Spaniards' complexion, and the women generally wear in one of the gristles of their noses a ring like a wedding ring, but somewhat greater, with a pearl and a Turkish stone set therein ; and this they do be they never so poor.

This is a place of very great traffic, and a very great thoroughfare from the East Indies to Aleppo. The town is very well furnished with victuals which come down the river of Tigris from Mosul, which was called Nineveh in old time[3]. They bring these victuals and divers sorts of merchandises upon rafts borne upon goats' skins blown up full of wind in manner of bladders ; and when they have discharged their goods they sell the rafts for fire and let the wind out of their goats' skins and carry them home again upon their asses by land, to make other voyages down the river[1].

The building here is most of brick dried in the Sun, and very little or no stone is to be found. Their houses are all flat-roofed and low. They have no rain for eight months together, nor almost any clouds in the sky night nor day. Their Winter is in November, December, January and February, which is as warm as our Summer in England, in a manner. This I know by good experience, because my abode at several times in this city of Babylon hath been at the least the space of two years. As we come to the city we pass over the river of Tigris on a great bridge, made with boats chained together with two mighty chains of iron[2].

Here is set a Letter of Master John Eldred to G. S.[3] Written in Bagdet the 14th day of July, 1583.

Right Worshipful,

My humble and hearty Commendations remembered ; wishing your health and desiring to hear of your prosperity, the which God increase and long continue, etc.

My last to you was in Aleppo, the 29th of May ; wherein I certified our arrival in the *Tiger* and the determining of this voyage ; how there was appointed to take at Aleppo, for the sum of two thousand pounds sterling, in Carsies[1], Cloths, Tin and other Commodities ; and with the same, Master Newbery, Ralph Fitch, Ralph Allen, William Skinner, William Shales and myself to go with the same goods to this place, there to leave two and part of the goods. At Balsara there leave two and part of the goods, and Master Newbery and Ralph Fitch to take for three or four hundred pounds sterling at Balsara of these goods and to go for the Indies.

Since which time, it may please you to understand, we all in company have come to this place ; and here arrived the 29th day of the last, having passed the hands of many bribing Dogs[2].

We arrived here all in safety, thanks be to God ; and whereas we had thought to have sold in this place great store of our commodities, we cannot sell, nor have not sold this sixteen days, for thirty Ducats, nor no likelihood of sales there until the Winter, this town is so full of Carsies and Tin ; most bought at Aleppo of William Barret, which were the Tin and Cloth that came in the *Emanuel*.

Tin is here as good cheap[1] as it is in Aleppo, and Cloth also. God send it to mend, or otherwise this Voyage of ours will make no profit. But in hope we rest the same will mend.

We have at this present embaled and laden aboard a Bark for Balsara : one hundred and twenty pieces of Carsies, half ; some Tin[2]; three Scarlets[3] ; eight and twenty Rotellos[4] of this place of Tin and Amber, with divers small Haberdash wares. Which is for the sum of seven hundred sixty-four pounds sterling. And here we leave the rest, which is about one thousand pounds, and with the same in this place we leave William Skinner and Ralph Allen, and all the rest of us go forward.

And at Balsara William Shales and myself do determine to stay to make sales and employment as the market will give us leave ; and Master Newbery and Ralph Fitch, with the Jeweller and Painter, are determined to proceed for the Indies. And out of this we carry to Balsara he will take out his four hundred pounds in Commodities for the Indies.

Thus the Lord bless our doings and send us a merry meeting in our Country[5], Norfolk, and that I may be your Servant, etc.

John Eldred.

And here a Letter of Master John Newbery to Master William Hareborne[1]*, Her Majesty's Ambassador to the Grand Signior*[2] *at Constantinople, communicated to Purchas*[3] *by Master John Sanderson. Bagdet, 15th July, 1583.*

Right Worshipful,

My hearty commendations premised, etc.

My last I sent you was of the 30th day of May last past, from Aleppo, and the next day after came from thence and the 19th day of the last month arrived at Feloge, the which is one day's journey from hence. Notwithstanding, some of our company came not thither until the last day of the last month (which was for want of camels to carry our goods), and since the goods came hither as yet have found but small sales; but towards Winter I hope it will be better. Notwithstanding, if I had money to put away with the Carsie we might have very good Spices; for with money there is here great good to be done, and without money there is no great profit made.

To-morrow I mean to go, with God's help, from hence to Balsara and so to Ormus; but my going to Ormus is more of necessity than for any goodwill I have to the place, for I want a man to go with me that hath the Indian tongue[4], the which is the only cause of my going thither for to take one there.

I was minded to have gone from Balsara by sea

to a place called Abowsher[1], and from thence by land into the Indies, but the want of one to speak for me[2] forceth me to leave that way. In Aleppo I hired two Naſtraynes[3], and one of them hath the Indian tongue and hath been twice there, but he and the other are so lewdly given[4] that it is not for me to truſt to either of them. One of them I leave here with Ralph Allen and William Skinner, and the other at Balsara with John Eldred and William Shales; and forced so to do, for that here is no other to be had, although I am in great doubt they will be a thousand Crowns hindrance to the Voyage, for that in divers matters of small value they have manifeſtly deceived us; but we put no more truſt in them, saving to speak for us. I was enforced to take them in Aleppo but two or three days before my coming from thence, or to have had none at all.

Here followeth the prices of Spices as they are worth here at this present:

Cloves and Maces, the Batman[5], five ducats;
Cinnamon, six ducats (and none to be had);
Nutmegs, forty-five Madynes;
Ginger, the Batman, one ducat;
Pepper, seventy-five Madynes; and
Silk (which is much better than that which cometh out of Persia), ducats eleven and a half the Batman.

And so, God preserve you.

In Babylon, this 15th day of July, 1583.

And here another Letter of Master Newbery, to the aforesaid Master Poore of London; written from Babylon the 20th July, 1583.

My last I sent you was the 29th of May last past, from Aleppo, by George Gill, the Purser of the *Tiger*, which[1] the last day of the same month came from thence and arrived at Feluge the 19th day of June; which Feluge is one day's journey from hence. Notwithstanding, some of our company came not hither till the last day of the last month, which was for want of Camels to carry our goods; for at this time of the year, by reason of the great heat that is here, Camels are very scant[2] to be gotten.

And since our coming hither we have found very small sales; but divers say that in the winter our commodities will be very well sold: I pray God their words may prove true. I think cloth, kerseys and tin have never been here at so low a price as they are now.

Notwithstanding, if I had here so much ready money as the commodities are worth I would not doubt to make a very good profit of this voyage hither and to Balsara, and so, by God's help, there will be reasonable profit made of the voyage. But with half money and half commodity may be bought here the best sort of spices and other commodities that are brought from the Indies, and without money there is here at this inſtant small good to be done.

With God's help, two days hence I mind to go from hence to Balsara, and from thence, of force, I must go to Ormus, for want of a man that speaketh the Indian tongue.

At my being in Aleppo I hired two Nazaranies, and one of them hath been twice in the Indies and hath the language very well, but he is a very lewd fellow and therefore I will not take him with me.

Here follow the prices of wares as they are worth here at this inſtant :

Cloves and maces, the bateman, 5 ducats ;

Cinnamon, 6 ducats (and few to be gotten) ;

Nutmegs, the bateman ; 45 medins (and 40 medins maketh a ducat) ;

Ginger, 40 medins ;

Pepper, 75 medins ;

Turbetta[1], the bateman, 50 medins ;

Neel[2], the churle[3], 70 ducats (and a churle is 27 rottils and a half of Aleppo) ;

Silk, much better than that which cometh from Persia, 11 ducats and a half the bateman (and every bateman here maketh 7 pound and 5 ounces English weight).

From Babylon, the 20th of July, 1583.

Yours,

John Newbery.

And here another of Master Newbery to the foresaid Master William Hareborne ; Balsara, the 15th August, 1583.

Right Worshipful,

My hearty commendations premised, etc.

My last I sent you was from Bagdet of the 16th day of the last month ; and the 22nd day of the same came from thence. But by reason that our Bark was great and the water very low, half-a-day's journey from thence came aground, and in a long time could not get her off again.

Whereupon, doubting that further below in the River we might be put to more trouble, I returned to the City and hired a smaller Boat, and the 27th day embarked our goods in the same Boat and the 6th day of this present arrived here. Since which time I have hired a Bark to go to Ormus, and within a day or two I mind, with God's help, to depart from hence.

About the beginning of this month arrived here four Venetians from Ormus, whereof three are for the account of Michael Stroopenny and the other for himself. Their Conducts[1] are twenty Bales of Turbith, Cloves and Cinnamon and Long-Pepper[2] and Musk, Pearls and Feathers ; which Feathers come from a City called Syndye[3], about one hundred and sixty leagues from Ormus, and are very much esteemed in Italy.

The Bashaw here hath taken away of their Feathers eighty-four thousand ; the which they say are worth a thousand ducats, and he would have given them five hundred and one ducats. So they say that they will certify of it to Constantinople, and hope to have some remedy from thence.

And if it were not sometimes for this kind of dealings by the Bashaw towards the Franks[1], here were in these countries very much good to be done ; for the exchange from Ormus to Aleppo is sixty per cento[2], and commonly they make their voyage in five or six months ; and if it were but only for the profit of the exchange it shall be good to have one remaining here and one at Ormus and another at Bagdet.

And to avoid all troubles that may happen either here or at Bagdet you shall do well to procure a commandment from the Grand Signior, both to the Bashaw of Bagdet and the Bashaw of this place, that and if any of our folks should die in this country (the which God forbid) that[3] the Bashaw neither any other Officer shall meddle with the goods, but that it may be kept in a Magosine within some Cave or Cravancera[4] until such time as the owners shall send for it, except there be more in company to take charge of the same. For here hath chanced Venetians to die, and although he were one that had nothing, and[5] he be in company with those that have great store of goods the Bashaw will take the goods and say that the goods did belong unto him that is dead ; and by this means they shall be in great trouble and leese[1] half their goods, if they can escape so. And if any of our company should die here, as God defend[2], the rest should be in great trouble about it.

As also that it may be in your commandment that it shall not be lawful for the Bashaw, or any other, for to take away from us any of our goods ; except he will pay for the same to our content. For many times there are fine things brought out of the Indies, and the Bashaw's man sitteth always in the Custom-house—especially at the coming of the Franks—and if there be anything that liketh him he taketh it and payeth for that which is worth a hundred pound, ten pound. And so the Bashaw hath dealt with many.

But if you send this commandment, that it may be registered both here and at Bagdet, it will for ever hereafter prevent those troubles that now we are in danger of ; and this is a thing very needful to be sent with those that shall next come hither.

There is as yet no Spaniards come into the Indies ; and by report of one that is here (who came from Ormus) there was a Spaniard sent out of Spain to Goa, to have had some authority there ; and the Viceroy caused him to be put to death, and will suffer none for to come thither[3].

As yet they alter not the keeping of their Christmas, as the Spaniards and others have done, but continue in keeping of their old reckoning of the Feasts and Months ; neither will they alter until commandment come from the Pope to the contrary.

And so I commit your Worship to God.

From Balsara, this 15th day of August, 1583.

Yours ever to command,

John Newbery.

Here is continued the Relation of Master John Eldred.

From thence we departed in flat-bottomed barks more strong and greater than those of Euphrates, and were eight and twenty days also in passing down this river to Balsara, but we might have done it in eighteen or less if the water had been higher. Upon the water's side stand by the way divers towns resembling much the names of the old prophets ; the first town they call Ozeah and another Zecchiah[1].

Before we come to Balsara, by one day's journey, the two rivers of Tigris and Euphrates meet, and there standeth a castle called Curna[2], kept by the Turks, where all merchants pay a small custom. Here the two rivers joined together begin to be eight or nine miles broad ; here also it beginneth to ebb and flow, and the water overflowing maketh the country all about very fertile of corn, rice, pulse and dates.

The town of Balsara is a mile and an half in circuit; all the buildings, Castle and walls are made of brick dried in the Sun. The Turk hath here five hundred Janissaries, besides other soldiers continually in garrison and pay, but his chief strength is of galleys, which are about five and twenty or thirty, very fair and furnished with goodly ordnance.

To this port of Balsara come monthly divers ships from Ormus, laden with all sorts of Indian merchandise, as spices, drugs, Indico[1] and Calecut[2] cloth. These ships are usually from forty to threescore tons, having their planks sewed together with cord made of the bark of Date-trees[3], and instead of Occam[4] they use the shiverings[5] of the bark of the said trees, and of the same they also make their tackling. They have no kind of iron-work belonging to these vessels, save only their anchors.

From this place, six days' sailing down the Gulf, they go to a place called Baharem[6] in the mid-way to Ormus; there they fish for pearls four months in the year, to wit, in June, July, August and September.

My abode in Balsara was just six months, during which time I received divers letters from Master John Newbery from Ormus, who as he passed that way with Her Majesty's letters to Zelabdim Echebar,

King of Cambaia, and unto the mighty Emperor of China, was traitorously there arrested, and all his company, by the Portugals, and afterward sent prisoner to Goa ; where, after a long and cruel imprisonment, he and his companions were delivered upon sureties not to depart the town without leave, at the suit of one Father Thomas Stevens, an English religious man which they found there. But shortly after three of them escaped, whereof one, to wit, Master Ralph Fitch, is since come into England. The fourth, which was a painter called John Story, became religious[1] in the College of St. Paul in Goa, as we understood by their letters.

Here are set two of those Letters whereof Master Eldred speaketh ; of which the first from Master Newbery at Ormus, to Master John Eldred and William Shales at Balsara ; the 21st September, 1583.

Right well beloved, and my assured good friends,

I heartily commend me unto you, hoping of your good healths, etc.

To certify you of my voyage after I departed from you time will not permit, but the 4th[2] of this present we arrived here, and the 10th day I with the rest were committed to prison, and about the middle of the next month the Captain[1] will send us all in his ship for Goa.

The cause why we are taken, as they say, is for that I brought letters from Don Antonio[2] ; but the truth is Michael Stropene was the only cause, upon letters that his brother wrote him from Aleppo.

God knoweth how we shall be dealt withal in Goa, and therefore if you can procure our Masters[3] to send the King of Spain his letters for our releasement you should do us great good, for they cannot, with justice, put us to death. It may be that they will cut our throats or keep us long in prison. God's will be done.

All those commodities that I brought hither had been very well sold if this trouble had not chanced. You shall do well to send with all speed a messenger by land from Balsara to Aleppo for to certify of this mischance (although it cost thirty or forty crowns), for that we may be the sooner released and I shall be the better able to recover this again, which is now like to be lost.

I pray you make my hearty commendations, etc.

From out of the prison in Ormus, this 21st of September, 1583.

John Newbery.

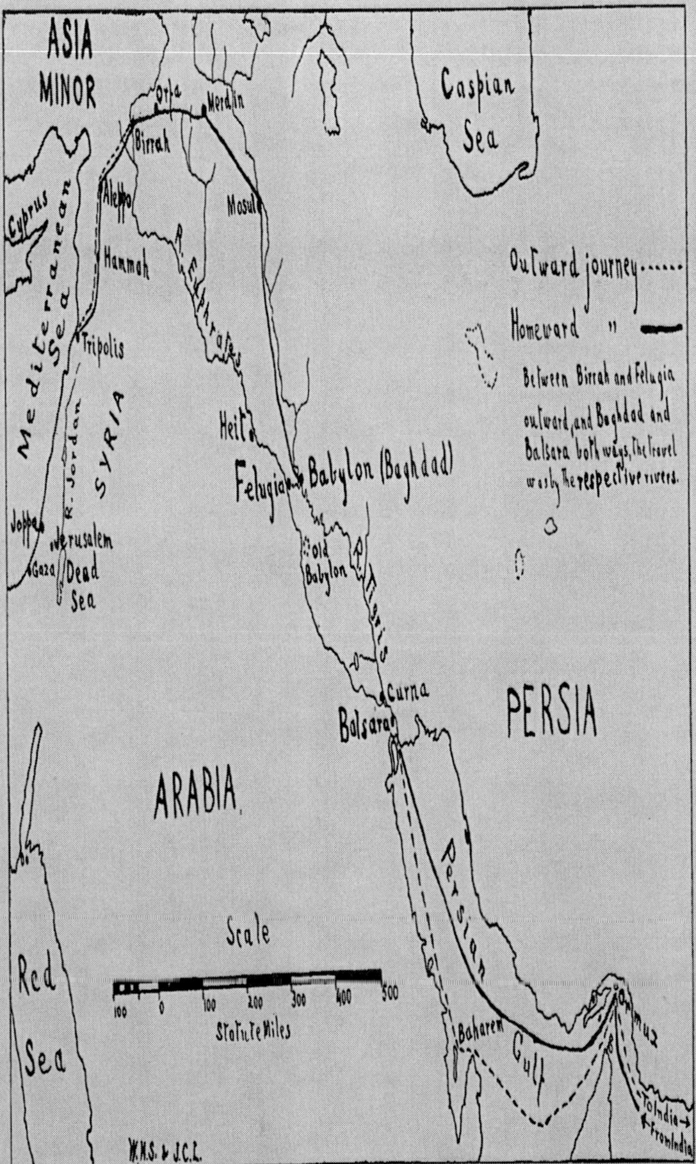

FITCH'S ROUTE BETWEEN TRIPOLIS AND ORMUZ, OUT AND HOME

[facing p. 60

And the second also from Master Newbery to Master John Eldred and William Shales, 24th September, 1583[1].

The bark of the Jews is arrived here two days past, by whom I know you did write ; but your letters are not like to come to my hands.

This bringer hath showed me here very great courtesy, wherefore I pray you show him what favour you may.

About the middle of the next month I think we shall depart from hence : God be our aid.

I think Andrew[2] will go by land to Aleppo ; wherein I pray you further him what you may. But if he should not go, then I pray you despatch away a messenger with as much speed as possibly[3] you may.

I can say no more ; but do for me as you would I should do for you in the like cause. And so with my very hearty commendations, etc.

From out of the prison in Ormus, this 24th day of September, 1583.

Yours, John Newbery.

And here a Letter of Master John Eldred and William Shales to G. S. From Balsara, the 6th of November, 1583.

Right Honourable,

Our humble duties considered, etc.

Our last unto your Lordship was from Babylon,

of the 19th of July; wherein we signified our safe arrival there and evil sales which we found, that in twenty days staying there we sold not for thirty Ducats.

Insomuch as by direction of Master Newbery we took of our commodities for seven hundred pounds sterling and came to this place Balsara; out of which Master Newbery took for the value of four hundred pounds and departed for Ormus, where he arrived the 4th of September and the 9th of the same was committed to Prison with all his Company—accused for Spies from Don Antonio, and that his Painter was to draw the plats[1] of Castles and Fortresses in the behalf of Don Antonio.

Whereupon the Captain of Ormus hath determined to send them, with the remainder of their goods which is unspent, Prisoners to Goa, there to be at the will and pleasure of the Vizrea[2]. What shall become of them, God knoweth.

He hath written to our worshipful Masters to procure the King of Spain his letters to the Vizrea of Goa for his delivery; which letters we have sent by messe express[3] to Aleppo. This his false accusation was by means of Venetians' Letters written from Aleppo and directed to Michael Stropennie in Ormus, who—as Master Newbery writeth—hath been the only cause of his trouble.

Concerning our eſtate[1], we have not sold, neither can sell, of all our Commodities for two hundred Ducats. Our Carsies here are not worn, neither come there any Merchants to make employments here ; being this place only as a thoroughfare[2] for Merchants which come from Ormus to discharge their goods and pay Cuſtom and so to pass for Babylon.

Before we came hither, Maſter Newbery told us we should find to make Bazar[3] for any kind of Spices ; which we have found clean contrary ; for neither are there Merchants resident here or Commodities to be found to make Bazar for two hundred Ducats. They which come from Ormus mindeth never to make Bazar here, but departeth[4] presently, after his Cuſtom paid, for Babylon.

We have offered to give our Commodities at price very reasonable, with as much money to have taken up the same by Exchange for Aleppo, but no man would deal with us. Whereupon we embarked our goods to have gone for Persia, but before our Ship's departure there arrived here two Venetians with divers sorts of Spices, who had taken up ten thousand ducats by Exchange to be paid here in Balsara. This money their credits will not serve to take up for Babylon ; insomuch as being in some diſtress for money they offered to barter with us, half money, half commodity ;

whereupon we have disbarked our goods, and hope within these few days to make Bazar with them.

Thus humbly taking our leaves, we cease to trouble your Lordship any further.

Your Lordship's most ready at commandment,

John Eldred.
William Shales.

And here another of Master John Eldred and William Shales to the foresaid G. S.; Balsara, the 22nd January, 1584.

Right Honourable,

Our duties humbly considered unto your Lordship, etc.

Our last was of the 10th of November, sent by the Cadie[1] of this place; wherein we signified unto your Lordship the alteration of our minds for going into Persia, and how we were returned with our goods back again to this place.

We also wrote you the hope which we had to make Bazar with a Frenchman which was at that time newly come from Ormus; the which is now come to pass and finished, although with some trouble. We delivered all our goods, which amounted unto two thousand Ducats, and gave him more in money two thousand, eight hundred and thirty Ducats, which we took up by Exchange for Bagdet at fifteen per Cento, and to pay more two per fifty per Month during the time of our staying here—which God knoweth how long it will be. The way between this place and Bagdet is full of Thieves, and no Merchants dare venture to depart till the ways be clear. There have gone no Barks from hence this four months and more.

We have embaled all our goods for Camels, being of them as followeth: four somes[1] of large Cinnamon; fourteen somes and an half of middle Cinnamon; three somes and an half of Nutmegs; one some and an half of Ginger; one some and a third part of Cloves; four somes and an half Fusses of Cloves[2]; an hundred and ninety-seven Turbands[3] (fine), and one Chest of gilded Pusillanes[4]. All these goods have been in readiness this month, wishing every day our departure; which God grant may be shortly, for here we spend and our money eateth, and that which is worse, we fear we shall lose our passage from Bagdet to Aleppo except we depart very shortly.

We received no Letters from Master Newbery since the first news of his trouble, but we hear by others that he and his Company are sent Prisoners to Goa and the remainder of his goods is left in the hands of the King's Factor.

Thus not having others[5] to trouble your Lordship

with at this present we reſt, humbly taking our leave, and commending you and all your Lordship's affairs to God's mighty protection,

Your Lordship's most ready at commandment till death,

John Eldred.
William Shales.

Here is continued the Relation of Maſter John Eldred.

I and my companion William Shales, having despatched our business at Balsara, embarked ourselves in company of seventy barks all laden with merchandise, having every bark fourteen men to draw them, like our Weſtern bargemen on the Thames ; and we were forty-four days coming up againſt the ſtream to Babylon. Where arriving and paying our cuſtom, we, with all other sorts of merchants, bought us camels, hired us men to lade and drive them, furnished ourselves with rice, butter, biscuit, honey made of dates, onions and dates ; and every merchant bought a proportion of live muttons[1] and hired certain shepherds to drive them with us. We also bought us tents to lie in and to put our goods under ; and in this our caravan were four thousand camels laden with spices and other rich merchandises. These camels will live very well two or three days without water ; their feeding is on thistles, wormwood, magdalene[1] and other strong weeds which they find upon the way. The government and deciding of all quarrels and duties to be paid, the whole caravan committeth to one special rich merchant of the company, of whose honesty they conceive best.

In passing from Babylon to Aleppo we spent forty days, travelling twenty or four and twenty miles a day ; resting ourselves commonly from two of the clock in the afternoon until three in the morning, at which time we begin to take our journey.

Eight days' journey from Babylon toward Aleppo, near unto a town called Heit[2] as we cross the river Euphrates by boats, about three miles from the town there is a valley wherein are many springs throwing out abundantly, at great mouths, a kind of black substance like unto tar, which serveth all the country to make staunch their barks and boats. Every one of these springs maketh a noise like unto a smith's forge in the blowing and puffing out of this matter, which never ceaseth night nor day, and the noise may be heard a mile off continually. This vale swalloweth up all heavy things that come upon it. The people of the country call it in their language " Babil gehenham ", that is to say, " Hell door "[3].

As we passed through these deserts we saw certain

wild beasts, as wild asses all white, roebucks, wolves, leopards, foxes and many hares, whereof we chased and killed many. Aborise[1], the King of the wandering Arabians in these deserts, hath a duty of forty shillings sterling upon every camel's load, which he sendeth his officers to receive of the Caravans ; and in consideration hereof he taketh upon him to conduct the said Caravans if they need his help and to defend them against certain prowling thieves.

I and my companion William Shales came to Aleppo with the Caravan the 11th of June, 1584, where we were joyfully received twenty miles distant from the town by Master William Barret our Consul, accompanied with his people and Janissaries ; who fell sick immediately and departed this life within eight days after, and elected before his death Master Anthony Bate Consul of our English nation in his place, who laudably supplied the same room three years.

In which mean time I made two voyages more unto Babylon and returned by the way aforesaid over the deserts of Arabia. And afterwards, as one desirous to see other parts of the country, I went from Aleppo to Antioch, which is thence sixty English miles, and from thence went down to Tripolis, where going abroad a small vessel I arrived at Joppa, and travelled to Rama, Lycia, Gaza, Jerusalem, Bethlehem, to the river of Jordan and the sea or lake of Sodom[2], and returned back to Joppa and from thence by sea to Tripolis ; of which places, because many others have published large discourses, I surcease to write. Within few days after, embarking myself at Tripolis the 22nd of December I arrived (God be thanked) in safety here in the river of Thames, with divers English merchants, the 26th of March, 1588, in the *Hercules* of London, which was the richest ship of English Merchants' goods that ever was known to come into this realm.

And so endeth the Relation of Master John Eldred.

Here beginneth the Voyage of Master Ralph Fitch, Merchant of London, by the way of Tripolis in Syria to Ormus, and so to Goa in the East India ; to Cambaia and all the kingdoms of Zelabdim Echebar the Great Mogor ; to the mighty river Ganges and down to Bengala[1] *; to Bacola and Chonderi*[2] *; to Pegu ; to Imahay in the kingdom of Siam and back to Pegu, and from thence to Malacca, Zeilan*[3]*, Cochin and all the coast of the East India. Begun in the year of our Lord 1583 and ended 1591 ; wherein the strange rites, manners and customs of those people, and the exceeding rich trade and commodities of those countries are faithfully set down and diligently described by the aforesaid Master Ralph Fitch.*

In the year of our Lord 1583, I, Ralph Fitch, of London, Merchant, being desirous to see the countries of the East India, in the company of Master John Newbery, Merchant (which had been at Ormus once before), of William Leedes, Jeweller, and James Story, Painter, being chiefly set forth[1] by the right worshipful Sir Edward Osborne, Knight, and Master Richard Staper, Citizens and Merchants of London, did ship myself in a ship of London called the *Tiger*, wherein we went for Tripolis in Syria and from thence we took the way for Aleppo, which we went in seven days with the Caravan. Being in Aleppo and finding good company we went from thence to Birra, which is two days and an half travel with Camels.

Birra is a little town, but very plentiful of victuals, and near to the wall of the town runneth the river of Euphrates. Here we bought a boat, and agreed with a Master and bargemen for to go to Babylon. These boats be but for one voyage, for the stream doth run so fast downwards that they cannot return. They carry you to a town which they call Felugia and there you sell the boat for a little money, for that which cost you fifty at Birra you sell there for seven or eight.

From Birra to Felugia is sixteen days' journey. It is not good that one boat go alone, for if it should chance to break you should have much ado to save your goods from the Arabians, which be always thereabouts robbing ; and in the night when your boats be made fast it is necessary that you keep good watch.

For the Arabians, that be thieves, will come swimming and steal your goods and flee away, against which a gun is very good, for they do fear it very much.

In the river of Euphrates, from Birra to Felugia, there be certain places where you pay custom, so many Medines for a some or Camel's lading, and certain raisins and soap, which is for the sons of Aborise which is Lord of the Arabians and all that great desert, and hath some villages upon the river. Felugia, where you unlade your goods which come from Birra, is a little village from whence you go to Babylon in a day.

Babylon is a town not very great, but very populous and of great traffic of strangers, for that it is the way to Persia, Turkia[1] and Arabia ; and from thence do go Caravans for these and other places. Here are great store of victuals, which come from Armenia down the river of Tigris. They are brought upon rafts made of goats' skins blown full of wind and boards laid upon them, and thereupon they lade their goods which are brought down to Babylon, which being discharged they open their skins and carry them back by Camels, to serve another time.

Babylon in times past did belong to the kingdom of Persia, but now is subject to the Turk. Over against Babylon there is a very fair village, from whence you pass to Babylon upon a long bridge made of boats and tied to a great chain of iron, which is made fast on either side of the river. When any boats are to pass up or down the river they take away certain of the boats until they be past.

The Tower of Babel is built upon this side the river Tigris, towards Arabia from the town about seven or eight miles[1] ; which tower is ruinated on all sides and with the fall thereof hath made, as it were, a little mountain, so that it hath no shape at all. It was made of bricks dried in the sun and certain canes and leaves of the palm-tree laid betwixt the bricks ; there is no entrance to be seen to go into it. It doth stand upon a great plain betwixt the rivers of Euphrates and Tigris.

By the river Euphrates, two days' journey from Babylon at a place called Ait[2], in a field near unto it, is a strange thing to see, a mouth that doth continually throw forth against the air boiling pitch with a fitting smoke, which pitch doth run abroad into a great field which is always full thereof. The Moors say that it is the Mouth of Hell. By reason of the great quantity of it the men of that country do pitch their boats two or three inches thick on the outside, so that no water doth enter into them. Their boats be called Danec. When there is great store of water in Tigris you may go from Babylon to Basora in eight or nine days ; if there be small store it will cost you the more days.

Basora in times past was under the Arabians but now is subject to the Turk. But some of them the

Turk cannot subdue, for that they hold certain Islands in the river Euphrates which the Turk cannot win of them. They be thieves all and have no settled dwelling, but remove from place to place with their Camels, goats and horses, wives and children and all. They have large blue gowns ; their wives' ears and noses are ringed very full of rings of copper and silver, and they wear rings of copper about their legs.

Basora standeth near the Gulf of Persia and is a town of great trade of spices and drugs, which come from Ormus. Also there is great store of wheat, rice and dates growing thereabout, wherewith they serve Babylon and all the country, Ormus and all the parts of India.

I went from Basora to Ormus down the Gulf of Persia in a certain ship made of boards and sewed together with cayro[1], which is thread made of the husk of cocoes, and certain canes or straw leaves sewed upon the seams of the boards, which is the cause that they leak very much. And so, having Persia always on the left hand and the coast of Arabia on the right hand, we passed many Islands, and among others the famous Island Baharim, from whence come the best pearls, which be round and Orient[2].

Ormus is an Island, in circuit about five and twenty or thirty miles, and is the dryest Island in the world, for there is nothing growing in it, but only salt. For their water, wood or victuals, and all things necessary, come out of Persia, which is about twelve miles from thence[1]. All the Islands thereabout be very fruitful, from whence all kind of victuals are sent unto Ormus. The Portugals have a Castle here which standeth near unto the sea, wherein there is a Captain for the King of Portugal, having under him a convenient number of soldiers, whereof some part remain in the Castle and some in the town.

In this town are merchants of all Nations and many Moors and Gentiles. Here is very great trade of all sorts of spices, drugs, silk, cloth of silk, fine tapestry of Persia[2], great store of pearls, which come from the Isle of Baharim and are the best pearls of all others, and many horses of Persia, which serve all India[3]. They have a Moor to their King, which is chosen and governed by the Portugals. Their women are very strangely attired, wearing on their noses, ears, necks, arms and legs many rings set with jewels, and locks[4] of silver and gold in their ears and a long bar of gold upon the side of their noses. Their ears, with the weight of their jewels, be worn so wide that a man may thrust three of his fingers into them[5].

Here, very shortly after our arrival, we were put in prison, and had part of our goods taken from us by the Captain of the Castle, whose name was Don Mathias de Albuquerque ; and from hence, the

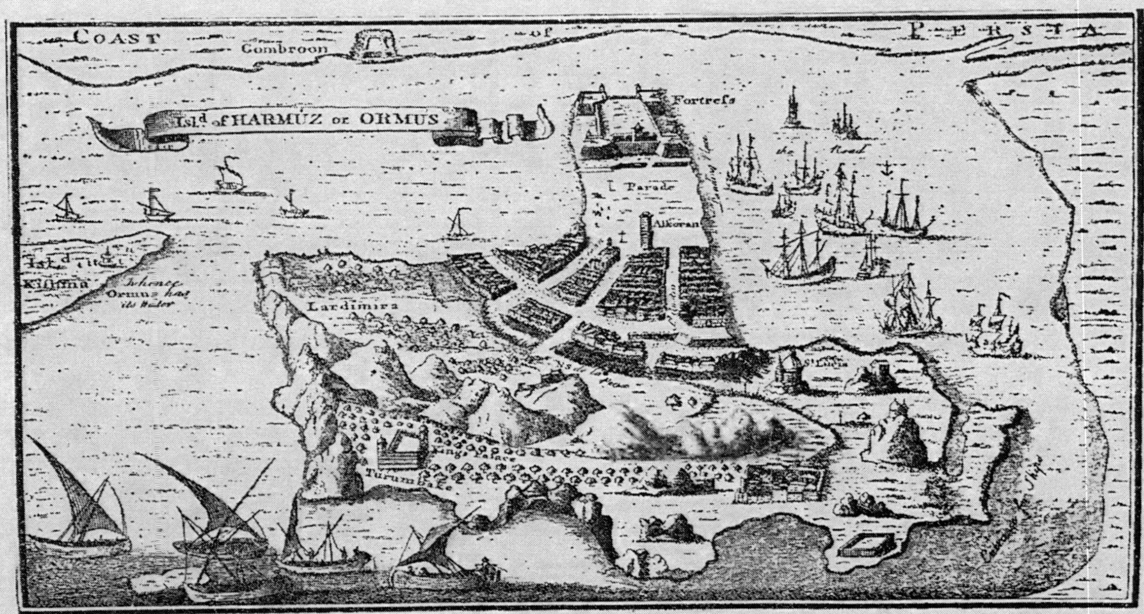

THE ISLAND AND TOWN OF ORMUS

[facing p. 74

11th of October, he shipped us and sent us for Goa unto the Viceroy, which at that time was Don Francisco de Mascarenhas.

The ship wherein we were embarked for Goa belonged to the Captain, and carried one hundred, twenty and four horses in it. All merchandise carried to Goa in a ship wherein are horses pay no custom to Goa. The horses pay custom, the goods pay nothing; but if you come in a ship which bringeth no horses you are then to pay eight in the hundred for your goods.

The first city of India that we arrived at upon the 5th of November, after we had passed the coast of Zindi[1], is called Diu[2], which standeth in an Island in the Kingdom of Cambaia and is the strongest town that the Portugals have in those parts. It is but little, but well stored with merchandise, for here they lade many great ships with divers commodities for the Straits of Mecca[3], for Ormus, and other places, and these be ships of the Moors and of Christians. But the Moors cannot pass except they have a passport from the Portugals.

Cambaietta[4] is the chief city of that province, which is great and very populous and fairly builded for a town of the Gentiles[5], but if there happen any famine the people will sell their children for very little[6]. The last king of Cambaia was Sultan Badu[7], which was killed at the siege of Diu, and shortly after his city was taken by the Great Mogor, which is the King of Agra and of Delli[1], which are forty days' journey from the country of Cambaia. Here the women wear upon their arms infinite numbers of rings made of elephants' teeth[2], wherein they take so much delight that they had rather be without their meat than without their bracelets.

Going from Diu we come to Daman[3], the second town of the Portugals in the country of Cambaia, which is distant from Diu forty leagues. Here is no trade but of corn and rice. They have many villages under them which they quietly possess in time of peace, but in time of war the enemy is master of them.

From thence we passed by Basaim[4] and from Basaim to Tana, at both which places is small trade but only of corn and rice.

The 10th of November we arrived at Chaul, which standeth in the firm land[5]. There be two towns, the one belonging to the Portugals and the other to the Moors. That of the Portugals is nearest to the sea and commandeth the bay, and is walled round about. A little above that is the town of the Moors, which is governed by a Moor King called Xa-Maluco[6]. Here is great traffic for all sorts of spices and drugs, silk and cloth of silk, sandals[7], elephants' teeth and much China work, and much sugar which is made of the nut called Gagara[8]; the tree is called the palmer,[9] which is the profitablest tree in the world. It doth always bear fruit, and doth yield wine, oil, sugar, vinegar, cords, coals ; of the leaves are made thatch for the houses, sails for ships, mats to sit or lie on ; of the branches they make their houses and brooms to sweep ; of the tree, wood for ships. The wine doth issue out of the top of the tree. They cut a branch of a bough and bind it hard and hang an earthen pot upon it, which they empty every morning and every evening and still[1] it and put in certain dried raisins, and it becometh very strong wine in short time[2].

Hither many ships come from all parts of India, Ormus and many from Mecca ; here be many Moors and Gentiles. They have a very strange order among them—they worship a cow and esteem much of the cow's dung to paint the walls of their houses[3]. They will kill nothing, not so much as a louse, for they hold it a sin to kill anything. They eat no flesh, but live by roots[4] and rice and milk. And when the husband dieth his wife is burned with him, if she be alive ; if she will not her head is shaven and then is never any account made of her after[5]. They say if they should be buried it were a great sin, for of their bodies there would come many worms and other vermin, and when their bodies were consumed those worms would lack sustenance, which were a sin ; therefore they will be burned. In Cambaia they will kill nothing nor have anything killed. In the town they have hospitals to keep lame dogs and cats, and for birds[1]. They will give meat[2] to the Ants.

Goa is the most principal city which the Portugals have in India[3], wherein the Viceroy remaineth with his court. It standeth in an Island, which may be twenty-five or thirty miles about. It is a fine city and, for an Indian town, very fair. The Island is very fair, full of orchards and gardens and many palmer trees, and hath some villages.

Here be many merchants of all nations, and the fleet which cometh every year from Portugal, which be four, five or six great ships, cometh first hither ; and they come for the most part in September and remain there forty or fifty days, and then go to Cochin[4], where they lade their pepper for Portugal. Oftentimes they lade one in Goa ; the rest go to Cochin, which is from Goa an hundred leagues southward[5]. Goa standeth in the country of Hidalcan, who lieth in the country six or seven days' journey ; his chief city is called Bisapor[6].

At our coming we were cast into the prison and examined before the Justice and demanded for letters, and were charged to be spies, but they could prove nothing by us. We continued in prison until the 22nd of December and then we were set at liberty, putting in sureties for two thousand ducats not to depart the town ; which sureties Father Stevens—an

GOA MARKET-PLACE

[*facing p.* 78

English Jesuit which we found there—and another religious man, a friend of his, procured for us.

Here is set a Letter of Master John Newbery to Master Leonard Poore; written from Goa, 20th January, 1584.

My last I sent you was from Ormus, whereby I certified you what had happened there unto me and the rest of my company, which was, that four days after our arrival there we were all committed to prison, except one Italian which came with me from Aleppo; whom the Captain never examined, only demanded what countryman he was. But I make account Michael Stropene, who accused us, had informed the Captain of him.

The first day we arrived there this Stropene accused us that we were spies sent from Don Antonio, besides divers other lies; notwithstanding, if we had been of any other country than of England we might freely have traded with them. And although we be Englishmen, I know no reason to the contrary but that we may trade hither and thither as well as other nations. For all nations do and may come freely to Ormus; as Frenchmen, Flemings, Almains[1], Hungarians, Italians, Greeks, Armenians, Nazaranies, Turks and Moors, Jews and Gentiles, Persians, Moscovites; and there is no nation that they seek for to trouble except ours. Wherefore it were contrary to all justice and reason that they should suffer all nations to trade with them and to forbid us.

But now I have as great liberty as any other nation, except it be to go out of the country, which thing as yet I desire not ; but I think hereafter (and before it be long) if I shall be desirous to go from hence, that they will not deny me licence.

Before we might be suffered to come out of prison I was forced to put in sureties for two thousand pardaus[1], not to depart from hence without licence of the Viceroy. Otherwise, except this, we have as much liberty as any other nation, for I have our goods again, and have taken an house in the chiefest street in the town, called the Rue Drette[2], where we sell our goods.

There were two causes which moved the Captain of Ormus to imprison us and afterward to send us hither. The first was because Michael Stropene had accused us of many matters which were most false ; and the second was for that Master Drake at his being at Maluco[3], caused two pieces of his ordnance to be shot at a galleon of the King's of Portugal, as they say.

But of these things I did not know at Ormus, and in the ship that we were sent in came the Chiefest Justice in Ormus, who was called Aveador General[4] of that place. He had been there three years, so that now his time was expired. Which Aveador is a great friend to the Captain of Ormus, who, certain days after our coming from thence, sent for me into his chamber and there began to demand of me many things (to the which I answered), and amongst the rest he said that Master Drake was sent out of England with many ships and came to Maluco and there laded cloves, and finding a galleon there of the King's of Portugal, he caused two pieces of his greatest ordnance to be shot at the same. And so, perceiving that this did greatly grieve them, I asked if they would be revenged of me for that which Master Drake had done. To the which he answered, No ; although his meaning was to the contrary.

He said, moreover, that the cause why the Captain of Ormus did send me for Goa was for that the Viceroy would understand of me what news there was of Don Antonio, and whether he were in England, yea or no ; and that it might be all for the best that I was sent hither, the which I trust in God will so fall out, although contrary to his expectation.

For had it not pleased God to put into the minds of the Archbishop and other two Padres or Jesuits of Saint Paul's College to stand our friends we might have rotted in prison. The Archbishop is a very good man, who hath two young men to his servants ; the one of them was born at Hamburgh and is called

Bernard Borgers, and the other was born at Enkhuisen, whose name is John Linscot[1], who did us great pleasure. For by them the Archbishop was many times put in mind of us.

And the two good Fathers of Saint Paul, who travailed very much for us, the one of them is called Padre Mark, who was born in Bruges in Flanders[2], and the other was born in Wiltshire in England and is called Padre Thomas Stevens.

Also I chanced to find here a young man who was born in Antwerp, but the most part of his bringing up hath been in London. His name is Francis de Rea, and with him it was my hap to be acquainted in Aleppo ; who also hath done me great pleasure here.

In the prison at Ormus we remained many days ; also we lay a long time at sea coming hither, and forthwith at our arrival here were carried to prison ; and the next day after were sent for before the Aveador—who is the Chiefest Justice—to be examined, and when we were examined he presently sent us back again to prison.

And after our being here in prison thirteen days, James Story went into the Monastery of Saint Paul, where he remaineth and is made one of the company ; which life he liketh very well.

And upon Saint Thomas's day[3] (which was twenty-two days after our arrival here) I came out of prison ;

and the next day after came out Ralph Fitch and William Bets.

If these troubles had not chanced I had been in possibility to have made as good a voyage as ever any man made with so much money. Many of our things I have sold very well, both here and at Ormus in prison. Notwithstanding the Captain willed me (if I would) to sell what I could before we embarked, and so with officers I went divers times out of the Castle in the morning and sold things and at night returned again to the prison. And all things that I sold they did write, and at our embarking from thence the Captain gave order that I should deliver all my money with the goods into the hands of the Scrivano, or Purser[1], of the ship, which I did, and the Scrivano made a remembrance,[2] which he left there with the Captain, that myself and the rest, with money and goods, he should deliver into the hands of the Aveador General of India. But at our arrival here the Aveador would neither meddle with goods nor money, for that he could not prove anything against us; wherefore the goods remained in the ship nine or ten days after our arrival, and then (for that the ship was to sail from thence) the Scrivano sent the goods on shore, and here they remained a day and a night and nobody to receive them.

In the end they suffered this bringer[3] to receive them (who came with me from Ormus) and put them into an[1] house which he had hired for me, where they remained four or five days. But afterward, when they should deliver the money, it was concluded by the Justice that both the money and the goods should be delivered into the positor's[2] hands, where they remained fourteen days after my coming out of prison.

At my being in Aleppo I bought a fountain of silver and gilt ; six knives ; six spoons, and one fork trimmed with coral, for five and twenty chekins, which the Captain of Ormus did take, and paid for the same twenty pardaos, which is one hundred larines, and was worth there or here, one hundred chekins. Also he had five emeralds set in gold, which were worth five hundred or six hundred crowns, and paid for the same an hundred pardaos[3]. Also he had nineteen and a half pikes[4] of cloth, which cost in London twenty shillings the pike, and was worth nine or ten crowns the pike, and he paid for the same twelve larines a pike. Also he had two pieces of green Kerseys, which were worth four and twenty pardaos the piece, and paid for them sixteen pardaos a-piece. Besides divers other trifles that the officers and others had in the like order, and some for nothing at all.

But the cause of all this was Michael Stropene[5], which came to Ormus not worth a penny and now hath thirty or forty thousand crowns ; and he grieveth that any other stranger should trade thither but himself.

But that shall not skill, for I trust in God to go both thither and hither, and to buy and sell as freely as he or any other.

Here is very great good to be done in divers of our commodities, and in like manner there is great profit to be made with commodities of this country, to be carried to Aleppo.

It were long for me to write, and tedious for you to read, of all things that have passed since my parting from you. But of all the troubles that have chanced since mine arrival in Ormus this bringer is able to certify you.

I mind to stay here ; wherefore, if you will write unto me, you may send your letters to some friend at Lisbon, and from thence by the ships they may be conveyed hither. Let the direction of your letters be either in Portuguese or Spanish, whereby they may come the better to my hands.

From Goa, this 20th day of January, 1584.

John Newbery.

And here a Letter written from Goa by Master Ralph Fitch to Master Leonard Poore abovesaid. 25th January, 1584.

Loving Friend, Master Poore, etc.

Since my departure from Aleppo I have not

written unto you any letters, by reason that at Babylon I was sick of the flux, and, being sick, I went from thence for Balsara (which was twelve days' journey down the river Tigris), where we had extreme hot weather (which was good for my disease), ill fare and worse lodging ; by reason our boat was pestered[1] with people.

In eight days, that which I did eat was very small, so that if we had stayed two days longer upon the water I think I had died ; but coming to Balsara, presently I mended, I thank God.

There we stayed fourteen days, and then we embarked ourselves for Ormus, where we arrived the 5th of September and were put in prison the 9th of the same month ; where we continued until the 11th of October and then were shipped for this city of Goa in the Captain's ship, with an hundred and fourteen horses and about two hundred men.

And passing by Diu and Chaul, where we went on land to water the 20th of November, we arrived at Goa the 29th of the same month ; where, for our better entertainment, we were presently put into a fair strong prison, where we continued until the 22nd of December.

It was the will of God that we found there two Padres, the one an Englishman, the other a Fleming. The Englishman's name is Padre Thomas Stevens ; the other's Padre Marco, of the Order of Saint Paul.

These did sue[1] for us unto the Viceroy and other officers, and stood us in as much stead as our lives and goods were worth ; for if they had not stuck to us, if we had escaped with our lives yet we had had long imprisonment.

After fourteen days' imprisonment they offered us, if we could put in sureties for two thousand ducats, we should go abroad in the town ; which when we could not do, the said Padres found sureties for us that we should not depart the country without the licence of the Viceroy.

It doth spite the Italians to see us abroad, and many marvel at our delivery. The painter is in the Cloister of Saint Paul, and is of their order and liketh there very well.

While we were in prison, both at Ormus and here, there was a great deal of our goods pilfered and lost, and we have been at great charges, in gifts and otherwise ; so that a great deal of our goods is consumed. There is much of our things which will sell very well, and some we shall get nothing for.

I hope in God that at the return of the Viceroy (which is gone to Chaul and Diu, they say, to win a castle of the Moors), whose return is thought will be about Easter, then we shall get our liberty and our sureties discharged. Then I think it will be our best way, either one or both, to return ; because our troubles have been so great and so much of our goods spoiled[1] and lost. But if it please God that I come into England, by God's help I will return hither again. It is a brave and pleasant country, and very fruitful. The summer is almost all the year long, but the chiefest at Christmas ; the day and the night are all of one length, very little difference, and marvellous great store of fruits.

For all our great troubles, yet are we fat and well-liking, for victuals are here plenty and good cheap.

And here I will pass over to certify you of strange things until our meeting, for it would be too long to write thereof. And thus I commit you to God, Who ever preserve you and us all.

From Goa in the East Indies, the 25th of January, 1584.

Yours to command,

Ralph Fitch.

Here is continued the Relation of Master Ralph Fitch.

Our surety's name was Andreas Taborer, to whom we paid 2,150 ducats and still he demanded more ; whereupon we made suit to the Viceroy and Justice to have our money again, considering that they had had it in their hands near five months and could prove nothing against us. The Viceroy made us a very sharp answer, and said we should be better sifted before it were long, and that they had further matter against us. Whereupon we presently determined rather to seek our liberties than to be in danger for ever to be slaves in the country, for it was told us we should have the strappado[1]. Whereupon presently, the fifth day of April, 1585, in the morning, we ran from thence, and being set over the river[2] we went two days on foot, not without fear; not knowing the way nor having any guide; for we durst trust none.

Here is set the Report of John Huighen van Linschoten concerning Master Newbery's and Master Fitch's imprisonment, and of their escape; which happened while he was in Goa.

In the month of December, Anno 1583, there arrived in the town and Island of Ormus four Englishmen; which came from Aleppo in the country of Syria, having sailed out of England and passed through the Straits of Gibraltar to Tripoli, a town and haven lying on the coast of Syria; where all the ships discharge their wares and merchandises, and from thence are carried by land unto Aleppo, which is nine days' journey.

In Aleppo there are resident divers merchants and factors of all nations, as Italians, Frenchmen, Englishmen, Armenians, Turks and Moors ; every man having his religion apart, paying tribute unto the Great Turk. In that town there is great traffic, for that from thence every year twice there travel two Caffyls[1], that is companies of people and camels, which travel unto India, Persia, Arabia, and all the countries bordering on the same, and deal in all sorts of merchandise both to and from those countries, as I in another place have already declared[2].

Three of the said Englishmen aforesaid were sent by the company of Englishmen that are resident in Aleppo to see if in Ormus they might keep any factors, and so traffic in that place like as also the Italians do, that is to say, the Venetians ; which in Ormus, Goa and Malacca have their factors and traffic there, as well for stones and pearls as for other wares and spices of those countries, which from thence are carried overland into Venice.

One of these Englishmen had been once before in the said town of Ormus[3], and there had taken good information of the trade ; and upon his advice and advertisement[4] the other were as then come thither with him, bringing great store of merchandises with them, as Cloths, Saffron, all kinds of drinking-glasses, and Haberdashers' wares, as looking-glasses, knives and suchlike stuff ; and, to conclude, brought with them all kind of small wares that may be devised.

And although those wares amounted unto great sums of money, notwithstanding, it was but only a shadow or colour, thereby to give no occasion to be mistrusted or seen into[1] ; for that their principal intent was to buy great quantities of precious stones, as Diamonds, Pearls, Rubies, etc., to the which end they brought with them a great sum of money and gold ; and that very secretly, not to be deceived[2] or robbed thereof, or to run into any danger for the same.

They, being thus arrived in Ormus, hired a shop and began to sell their wares ; which the Italians perceiving (whose factors continue there, as I said before), and fearing that those Englishmen—finding good vent for their commodities in that place—would be resident therein and so daily increase, which would be no small loss and hindrance unto them, did presently invent all the subtle means they could to hinder them.

And to that end they went unto the Captain of Ormus, as then called Don Gonsalo de Meneses,[3] telling him that there were certain Englishmen come into Ormus that were sent only to spy the country ; and said, further, that they were heretics ; and therefore, they said, it was convenient they should not be suffered so to depart without being examined and punished as enemies, to the example of others.

The Captain, being a friend unto the Englishmen by reason that one of them which had been there before had given him certain presents, would not be persuaded to trouble them, but shipped them with all their wares in a ship that was to sail for Goa, and sent them to the Viceroy that he might examine and try them as he thought good. Where, when they were arrived, they were cast into prison, and first examined whether they were good Christians or no. And because they could speak but bad Portugal, only two of them spake good Dutch (as having been certain years in the Low Countries and there trafficked), there was a Dutch Jesuit born in the town of Bruges in Flanders, that had been resident in the Indies for thirty years, sent unto them to undermine and examine them: wherein they behaved themselves so well that they were holden and esteemed for good and Catholic Christians, yet still suspected because they were strangers, and especially Englishmen.

The Jesuits still[1] told them that they should be sent prisoners into Portugal, wishing them to leave off their trade of merchandise and to become Jesuits, promising them thereby to defend them from all trouble. The cause why they said so and persuaded them in that earnest manner was for that the Dutch Jesuit had secretly been advertised of great sums of money which they had about them, and sought to get the same into their fingers; for that the first vow and promise they make at their entrance into their Order is to procure the welfare of their said Order, by what means soever it be.

But although the Englishmen denied them, and refused the Order, saying that they were unfit for such places, nevertheless they proceeded so far that one of them, being a Painter (that came with the other three for company, to see the countries and to seek his fortune, and was not sent thither by the English merchants), partly for fear and partly for want of means to relieve himself, promised them to become a Jesuit. And although they knew and well perceived he was not any of those that had the treasure, yet because he was a Painter (whereof there are but few in India) and that they had great need of him to paint their church, which otherwise would coſt them great charges to bring one from Portugal, they were very glad thereof, hoping in time to get the reſt of them, with all their money, into their fellowship. So that, to conclude, they made this Painter a Jesuit, where he continued certain days ; giving him good ſtore of work to do and entertaining him with all the favour and friendship they could devise, and all to win the reſt to be a prey for them.

But the other three continued ſtill in prison, being in great fear because they underſtood no man that came to them, nor any man almoſt knew what they said ; till in the end it was told them that certain Dutchmen dwelt in the Archbishop's house and counsel given them to send unto them.

Whereat they much rejoiced, and sent to me and another Dutchman, desiring us once to come and speak with them, which we presently did. And they with tears in their eyes made complaint unto us of their hard usage, showing us from point to point (as it is said before) why they were come into the country ; withal desiring us, for God's cause, if we might by any means, to help them, that they might be set at liberty upon sureties, being ready to endure what Justice should ordain for them ; saying that if it were found contrary, and that they were other than travelling merchants and sought to find out further benefit by their wares, they would be content to be punished.

With that we departed from them, promising them to do our best ; and in the end we obtained so much of the Archbishop that he went unto the Viceroy to deliver our petition, and persuaded him so well that he was content to set them at liberty, and that their goods should be delivered unto them again ; upon condition they should put in sureties for two thousand pardawes, not to depart the country before other order should be taken with them.

Thereupon they presently found a Citizen of the town that was their surety for two thousand pardawes, to whom they paid in hand one thousand and three

CIVIL AND MILITARY COSTUMES OF THE PORTUGUESE IN GOA

facing p. 94

hundred pardawes, and, because they said they had no more ready money, he gave them credit, seeing what ﬅore of merchandise they had ; whereby at all times, if need be, he might be satisfied. And by that means they were delivered out of prison and hired themselves an house and began to set open shop ; so that they uttered[1] much ware and were presently well known among all the merchants, because they always respected[2] gentlemen (specially such as bought their wares), showing great courtesy and honour unto them; whereby they won much credit and were beloved of all men, so that every man favoured them and was willing to do them pleasure.

To us they showed great friendship, for whose sake the Archbishop favoured them much and showed them very good countenance ; which they knew well how to increase by offering him many presents, although he would not receive them, neither would ever take gift or present at any man's hands.

Likewise they behaved themselves so discreetly that no man carried an evil eye—no, nor an evil thought—towards them. Which liked not the Jesuits, because it hindered them from that they hoped for.

So that they ceased not ﬅill, by this Dutch Jesuit, to put them in fear that they should be sent into Portugal to the King, counselling them to yield themselves Jesuits into their Cloiﬅer ; which if they did, he said they would defend them from all troubles ; saying further, that he counselled them therein as a friend and one that knew for certain that it was so determined by the Viceroy's Privy Council ; which to effect, he said, they stayed but for shipping that should sail for Portugal ; with divers other persuasions to put them in some fear and so to effect their purpose.

The Englishmen to the contrary durst not say anything to them, but answered that as yet they would stay a while and consider thereof ; thereby putting the Jesuits in comfort. As one among them, being the principal of them (called John Newbery), complained, unto me oftentimes ; saying that he knew not what to say or think therein, or which way he might be rid of those troubles.

But in the end they determined with themselves to depart from thence ; and secretly, by means of other friends, they employed their money in precious stones, which the better to effect one was a Jeweller and for the same purpose came with them. Which, being concluded among them, they durst not make known to any man, neither did they credit us so much as to show us their minds therein, although they told us all whatsoever they knew. But on a Whit Sunday they went abroad to sport[1] themselves about three miles from Goa, in the mouth of the river in a country called Bardes[2], having with them good store of meat and drink. And because they should not be suspected, they left their house and shop, with some wares therein unsold, in custody of a Dutch boy—by us provided for them—that looked unto it. This boy was in the house, not knowing their intent.

And being in Bardes, they had with them a Patamar[1], which is one of the Indian posts which in the Winter times carrieth letters from one place to the other, whom they had hired to guide them ; and because that between Bardes and the firm land there is but a little river, in a manner half dry, they passed over it on foot and so travelled by land, being never heard of again. But it is thought they arrived in Aleppo, as some say, but they know not certainly. Their greatest hope was that John Newbery could speak the Arabian tongue, which is used in all those countries[2], or at the least understood ; for it is very common in all places thereabouts, as French with us.

News being come to Goa, there was a great stir and murmuring among the people, and we much wondered at it ; for many were of opinion that we had given them counsel so to do. And presently their surety seized upon the goods remaining, which might amount unto above two hundred pardawes, and with that and the money he had received of the Englishmen he went unto the Viceroy and delivered it unto him ; which the Viceroy having received, forgave him the rest.

This flight of the Englishmen grieved the Jesuits most, because they had lost such a prey ; which they made sure account of. Whereupon the Dutch Jesuit came to us to ask us if we knew thereof, saying that if he had suspected so much he would have dealt otherwise. For that, he said, he once had in his hands of theirs a bag wherein was forty thousand Veneseanders (each Veneseander being two pardawes)[1], which was when they were in prison, and that they had always put him in comfort to accomplish his desire. Upon the which promise he gave them their money again, which otherwise they should not so lightly have come by, or peradventure never, as he openly said. And in the end he called them heretics and spies, with a thousand other railing speeches which he uttered against them.

The Englishman that was become a Jesuit, hearing that his companions were gone and perceiving that the Jesuits showed him not so great favour, neither used him so well as they did at the first, repented himself. And seeing he had not as then made any solemn promise, and being counselled to leave the House and told that he could not want a living in the town, as also that the Jesuits could not keep him there without he were willing to stay (so they could not accuse him of anything), he told them flatly that he had no desire to stay within the Cloister. And although they used all the means they could to keep him there yet he would not stay, but hired an house without the Cloister and opened shop, where he had good store of work. And in the end married a Mestizo's[1] daughter of the town, so that he made his account to stay there while he lived.

By this Englishman I was instructed of all the ways, trades and voyages of the country between Aleppo and Ormus, and of all the ordinances and common customs which they usually hold during their voyage over the land ; as also of the places and towns where they passed.

And since those Englishmen's departures from Goa there never arrived any strangers, either English or others, by land in the said countries[2], but only Italians, which daily traffic overland and use continual trade, going and coming, that way.

Which concludeth this Report.

And here continueth the Relation of Master Ralph Fitch.

One of the first towns which we came unto is called Bellergan[3], where there is a great market kept of Diamonds, Rubies, Sapphires and many other soft stones[4]. From Bellergan we went to Bisapor, which is a very great town where the King doth keep his court. He hath many Gentiles in his court and they be great idolators, and they have their idols standing in the woods, which they call Pagodes[1]. Some be like a cow, some like a monkey, some like buffles[2], some like peacocks and some like the devil. Here be very many elephants, which they go to war withal. Here they have good store of gold and silver ; their houses are of stone, very fair and high.

From hence we went for Gulconda, the king whereof is called Cutup de lashach[3]. Here and in the kingdom of Hidalcan, and in the country of the king of Deccan[4], be the Diamonds found of the old water[5]. It is a very fair town, pleasant, with fair houses of brick and timber ; it aboundeth with great store of fruits and fresh water. Here the men and the women do go with a cloth bound about their middles without any more apparel. We found it here very hot ; the winter[6] beginneth here about the last of May.

In these parts is a port or haven called Masulipatan[7], which standeth eight days' journey hence toward the gulf of Bengala, whither come many ships out of India, Pegu and Sumatra, very richly laden with pepper, spices and other commodities. The country is very good and fruitful. From thence I went to Servidore, which is a fine country and the King is called the King of Bread[8]. The houses here be all thatched and made of loam.[1] Here be many Moors and Gentiles, but there is small religion among them.

From thence I went to Bellapore[2] and so to Barrampore[3], which is in the country of Zelabdim Echebar. In this place their money is made of a kind of silver, round and thick, to the value of twenty pence ; which is very good silver[4]. It is a marvellous great and populous country. In their winter, which is in June, July and August, there is no passing in the streets but with horses, the waters be so high. The houses are made of loam and thatched. Here is great store of cotton cloth made and painted cloths[5] of cotton-wool[6]. Here groweth great store of corn and rice.

We found marriages great store, both in towns and villages in many places where we passed, of boys of eight or ten years and girls of five or six years old. They both do ride upon one horse, very trimly decked, and are carried through the town with great piping and playing, and so return home and eat of a Banquet made of rice and fruits ; and there they dance the most part of the night and so make an end of the marriage. They lie not together until they be ten years old. They say they marry their children so young because it is an order that when the man dieth the woman must be burned with him ; so that if the father die yet they may have a father-in-law to help to bring up the children which be married ; and also that they will not leave their sons without wives nor their daughters without husbands.

From thence we went to Mandoway[1], which is a very strong town. It was besieged twelve years by Zelabdim Echebar before he could win it. It standeth upon a very great high rock, as the most part of their castles do, and was of a very great circuit. From hence we went to Ugini and Serringe[2], where we overtook the Ambassador of Zelabdim Echebar with a marvellous great company of men, elephants and camels. Here is great trade of cotton and cloth made of cotton, and great store of drugs. From thence we went to Agra, passing many rivers, which by reason of the rain were so swollen that we waded and swam oftentimes for our lives.

Agra is a very great city and populous, built with stone, having fair and large streets; with a fair river running by it which falleth into the Gulf of Bengala. It hath a fair castle and a strong, with a very fair ditch. Here be many Moors and Gentiles. The King is called Zelabdim Echebar; the people for the most part call him The Great Mogor.

From thence we went for Fatepore[3], which is the place where the King kept his court. The town is greater than Agra, but the houses and streets be not so fair. Here dwell many people, both Moors and Gentiles.

The King hath in Agra and Fatepore, as they do credibly report, a thousand Elephants, thirty thousand Horses, fourteen hundred tame Deer, eight hundred Concubines ; such store of Ounces, Tigers, Buffles, Cocks and Hawks that is very strange to see. He keepeth a great court, which they call Derrican[1].

Agra and Fatepore are two very great cities, either of them much greater than London and very populous. Between Agra and Fatepore are twelve miles[2], and all the way is a market of victuals and other things, as full as though a man were still in a town and so many people as if a man were in a market. They have many fine carts—and many of them carved and gilded with gold—with two wheels, which be drawn with two little Bulls about the bigness of our great dogs in England, and they will run with any horse and carry two or three men in one of these carts ; they are covered with silk or very fine cloth, and be used here as our coaches be in England.

Hither is great resort of merchants from Persia and out of India[3], and very much merchandise of silk and cloth and of precious stones, both Rubies, Diamonds and Pearls. The King is apparelled in a white Cabie[4] made like a shirt, tied with strings on the one side, and a little cloth on his head coloured oftentimes with red or yellow. None come into his house but his eunuchs, which keep his women.

Here in Fatepore we stayed all three until the 28th of September, 1585, and then Master John Newbery took his journey toward the city of Lahore, determining from thence to go for Persia and then for Aleppo or Constantinople, whether[1] he could get soonest passage unto, and directed me to go for Bengala and for Pegu and did promise me, if it pleased God, to meet me in Bengala within two years with a ship out of England.

I left William Leedes, the jeweller, in service with the king, Zelabdim Echebar, in Fatepore, who did entertain him very well and gave him an house and five slaves, an horse and every day six shillings in money.

I went from Agra to Satagam[2] in Bengala, in the company of one hundred and fourscore boats, laden with Salt, Opium, Hinge[3], Lead, Carpets and divers other commodities, down the river Jemena[4]. The chief merchants are Moors and Gentiles.

In these countries they have many strange ceremonies. The Bramanes, which are their priests, come to the water and have a string[5] about their necks made with great ceremonies, and lade up water with both their hands and turn the string first with both their hands within and then one arm after the other out. Though it be never so cold they will wash themselves in cold water or in warm.

These Gentiles will eat no flesh nor kill anything. They live with rice, butter, milk and fruits. They pray in the water naked, and dress their meat[1] and eat it naked, and for their penance they lie flat upon the earth and rise up and turn themselves about thirty or forty times, and use to heave up their hands to the sun and to kiss the earth, with their arms and legs stretched along out, and their right leg always before the left. Every time they lie down they make a score on the ground with their finger, to know when their stint[2] is finished.

The Bramanes mark themselves in the foreheads, ears and throats with a kind of yellow gear which they grind[3], and every morning they do it. And they have some old men which go in the streets with a box of yellow powder and mark men on their heads and necks as they meet them. And their wives do come by ten, twenty and thirty together to the water-side singing, and there do wash themselves and then use their ceremonies and mark themselves in their foreheads and faces, and carry some with them and so depart singing.

Their daughters be married at or before the age of ten years. The men may have seven wives. They be a kind of crafty people, worse than the Jews. When they salute one another they heave up their hands to their heads and say Rame, Rame[4].

From Agra I came to Prage[1], where the river Jemena entereth into the mighty river Ganges and Jemena loseth his name. Ganges cometh out of the North-west and runneth East into the Gulf of Bengala. In those parts there are many tigers, and many partridges and turtle-doves and much other fowl.

Here be many beggars in these countries which go naked, and the people make great account of them ; they call them Schesche[2]. Here I saw one which was a monster[3] among the rest. He would have nothing upon him, his beard was very long, and with the hair of his head he covered his privities. The nails of some of his fingers were two inches long, for he would cut nothing from him, neither would he speak. He was accompanied with eight or ten and they spake for him. When any man spake to him he would lay his hand upon his breast and bow himself, but would not speak. He would not speak to the King.

We went from Prage down Ganges, the which is here very broad. Here is great store of fish of sundry sorts and of wild-fowl, as of swans, geese, cranes, and many other things. The country is very fruitful and populous. The men, for the most part, have their faces shaven and their heads[4] very long, except some which be all shaven save the crown ; and some of them are as though a man should set a dish on their heads and shave them round, all but the crown. In this river of Ganges are many Islands ; his water is very sweet and pleasant and the country adjoining very fruitful.

From thence we went to Bannaras[1], which is a great town, and great store of cloth is made there of cotton, and Shashes[2] for the Moors. In this place they be all Gentiles, and be the greatest idolators that ever I saw.

To this town come the Gentiles on pilgrimage out of far countries. Here alongst[3] the water's side be very many fair houses, and in all of them, or for the most part, they have their images standing, which be evil-favoured, made of stone and wood ; some like lions, leopards and monkeys, some like men and women and peacocks, and some like the devil with four arms and four hands ; they sit cross-legged, some with one thing in their hands and some another, and by break of day and before there are men and women which come out of the town and wash themselves in Ganges.

And there are divers old men which upon places of earth made for the purpose sit praying, and they give the people three or four straws[4], which they take and hold them between their fingers when they wash themselves. And some sit to mark them in the foreheads, and they have in a cloth a little rice, barley or money, which, when they have washed themselves, they give to the old men which sit there praying. Afterwards they go to divers of their images and give them of their sacrifices ; and when they give the old men say certain prayers, and then is all holy.

And in divers places there standeth a kind of image which in their language they call Ada ; and they have divers great stones carved, whereon they pour water and throw thereupon some rice, wheat, barley and some other things. This Ada hath four hands with claws[1].

Moreover, they have a great place made of stone, like to a well with steps to go down, wherein the water standeth very foul and stinketh ; for the great quantity of flowers which continually they throw into it do make it stink. There be always many people in it ; for they say when they wash themselves in it that their sins be forgiven them, because God, as they say, did wash himself in that place[2]. They gather up the sand in the bottom of it and say it is holy.

They never pray but in the water, and they wash themselves overhead, and lade up water with both their hands, and turn themselves about ; and then they drink a little of the water three times, and so go to their gods which stand in those houses.

Some of them will wash a place which is their length, and then will pray upon the earth with their arms and legs at length out, and will rise up and lie down, and kiss the ground twenty or thirty times, but they will not stir their right foot[1]. And some of them will make their ceremonies with fifteen or sixteen pots, little and great, and ring a little bell, when they make their mixtures, ten or twelve times ; and they make a circle of water round about their pots and pray. And divers sit by them, and one that reacheth them their pots, and they say divers things over their pots many times, and when they have done they go to their gods and strew their sacrifices, which they think are very holy, and mark many of them which sit by in the foreheads, which they take as a great gift.

There come fifty and sometimes an hundred together, to wash them in this well and to offer to these idols.

They have in some of these houses their idols standing, and one sitteth by them in warm weather with a fan to blow wind upon them. And when they see any company coming they ring a little bell[2] which hangeth by them and many give them their alms, but especially those which come out of the country. Many of them are black and have claws of brass with long nails, and some ride upon peacocks and other fowls which be evil-favoured with long hawk's bills ; and some like one thing and some another, but none with a good face. Among the rest, there is one which they make great account of, for they say he giveth them all things, both food and apparel, and one sitteth always by him with a fan to make wind towards him.

Here some be burned to ashes, some scorched in the fire and thrown into the water, and dogs and foxes do presently eat them. The wives here do burn with their husbands when they die; if they will not, their heads be shaven and never any account is made of them afterward.

The people go all naked save a little cloth bound about their middle. Their women have their necks, arms and ears decked with rings of silver, copper, tin, and with round hoops made of Ivory, adorned with amber stones and with many agates, and they are marked with a great spot of red in their foreheads and a great stroke of red up to the crown, and so it runneth three manner of ways. In their winter, which is our May, the men wear quilted gowns of cotton like to our mattresses, and quilted caps like to our great grocers' mortars, with a slit to look out at, and so tied down beneath their ears.

If a man or woman be sick and like to die they will lay him before their idols all night, and that shall help him or make an end of him. And if he do not mend that night his friends will come and sit with him a little and cry, and afterwards will carry him to the water's side and set him upon a little raft made of reeds, and so let him go down the river.

When they be married the man and the woman come to the water-side, and there is an old man which they call a Bramane (that is, a priest), a cow and a calf, or a cow with calf. Then the man and the woman, cow and calf, and the old man, go into the water together, and they give the old man a white cloth of four yards long and a basket, cross-bound, with divers things in it. The cloth he layeth upon the back of the cow and then he taketh the cow by the end of the tail and sayeth certain words. And she hath a copper or a brass pot full of water, and the man doth hold his hand by the old man's hand, and the wife's hand by her husband's, and all have the cow by the tail; and they pour water out of the pot upon the cow's tail and it runneth through all their hands and they lade up water with their hands; and then the old man doth tie him and her together by their clothes. Which done, they go round about the cow and calf, and then they give somewhat to the poor which be always there, and to the Bramane or priest they give the cow and calf, and afterward go to divers of their idols and offer money, and lie down flat upon the ground and kiss it divers times, and then go their way[1].

Their chief idols be black and evil-favoured; their mouths monstrous, their ears gilded and full of jewels, their teeth and eyes of gold, silver and glass, some having one thing in their hands and some another. You may not come into the houses where they stand with your shoes on. They have continually lamps burning before them.

From Bannaras I went to Patenaw[1] down the river of Ganges, where in the way we passed many fair towns and a country very fruitful. And many very great rivers do enter into Ganges, and some of them as great as Ganges, which cause Ganges to be of a great breadth, and so broad that in the time of rain you cannot see from one side to the other.

These Indians, when they be scorched and thrown into the water, the men swim with their faces downwards, the women with their faces upwards. I thought they tied something to them to cause them to do so, but they say no.

There be very many thieves in this country; which be like to the Arabians, for they have no certain abode, but are sometime in one place and sometime in another[2].

Here the women be so decked with silver and copper that it is strange to see; they use no shoes by reason of the rings of silver and copper which they wear on their toes.

Here at Patenaw they find gold in this manner. They dig deep pits in the earth and wash the earth in great bowls, and therein they find the gold; and they make the pits round about with brick, that the earth fall not in.

Patenaw is a very long and a great town. In times past it was a kingdom, but now it is under Zelabdim Echebar, the Great Mogor[1]. The men are tall and slender, and have many old folks among them. The houses are simple, made of earth and covered with straw; the streets are very large.

In this town there is a trade of cotton and cloth of cotton; much sugar, which they carry from hence to Bengala and India; very much opium and other commodities. He that is chief here under the King is called Tipperdas, and is of great account among the people.

Here in Patenaw I saw a dissembling prophet, which sat upon an horse in the market-place and made as though he slept; and many of the people came and touched his feet with their hands and then kissed their hands. They took him for a great man, but sure he was a lazy lubber. I left him there sleeping. The people of these countries be much given to such prating and dissembling hypocrites.

From Patenaw I went to Tanda[2], which is in the land of Gouren. It hath in times past been a kingdom, but now is subdued by Zelabdim Echebar. Great trade and traffic is here of cotton and of cloth of cotton. The people go naked, with a little cloth bound about their waiſt. It ſtandeth in the country of Bengala.

Here be many tigers, wild bufs and great ſtore of wild fowl. They are very great idolators. Tanda ſtandeth from the river Ganges a league, because in times paſt the river, flowing over the banks in time of rain, did drown the country, and many villages, and so they do remain ; and the old way which the river Ganges was wont to run remaineth dry, which is the occasion that the city doth ſtand so far from the water. From Agra, down the river Jemena and down the river Ganges, I was five months coming to Bengala, but it may be sailed in much shorter time.

I went from Bengala into the country of Couche, which lieth twenty-five days' journey northwards from Tanda. The King is a Gentile ; his name is Suckel Counse[1]. His country is great and lieth not far from Cauchin China, for they say they have pepper from thence. The port is called Cacchegate[2]. All the country is set with Bambos or Canes, made sharp at both the ends and driven into the earth, and they can let in the water and drown the ground above knee-deep, so that men nor horses can pass. They poison all the waters if any wars be.

Here they have much silk and musk, and cloth made of cotton. The people have ears which be marvellous great, of a span long, which they draw out in length by devices when they be young.

Here they be all Gentiles and they will kill nothing. They have hospitals for sheep, goats, dogs, cats, birds, and for all other living creatures ; when they be old and lame they keep them until they die. If a man catch or buy any quick thing in other places and bring it thither, they will give him money for it or other victuals and keep it in their hospitals or let it go. They will give meat to the ants. Their small money is almonds[1], which oftentimes they use to eat.

From thence I returned to Hugeli[2], which is the place where the Portugals keep[3] in the country of Bengala, which standeth in 23 degrees of northerly latitude and standeth a league from Satagan (they call it Porto Piqueno)[4]. We went through the wilderness, because the right way[5] was full of thieves, where we passed the country of Gouren ; where we found but few villages but almost all wilderness, and saw many buffes, swine and deer, grass longer than a man, and very many Tigers.

Not far from Porto Piqueno, South-westward, standeth an haven which is called Angeli, in the country of Orixa[6]. It was a kingdom of itself and the king was a great friend to strangers. Afterwards it was taken by the King of Patan, which was their neighbour ; but he did not enjoy it long, but was taken by Zelabdim Echebar, which is King of Agra, Delli and Cambaia. Orıxa ﬅandeth six days' journey from Satagam, South-weﬅward.

In this place is very much rice and cloth made of cotton ; and great ﬅore of cloth which is made of grass, which they call Yerva[1] ; it is like a silk. They make good cloth of it, which they send for India and divers other places. To this haven of Angeli come every year many ships out of India, Negapatan, Sumatra, Malacca and divers other places, and lade from thence great ﬅore of rice and much cloth of cotton-wool ; much sugar and long pepper ; great ﬅore of butter and other viƈtuals for India.

Satagam is a fair city for a city of the Moors, and very plentiful of all things. Here in Bengala they have every day in one place or other a great market which they call Chandeau[2], and they have many great boats which they call pericose[3], wherewithal they go from place to place and buy rice and many other things. These boats have twenty-four or twenty-six oars to row them ; they be great of burden but have no coverture[4]. Here the Gentiles have the water of Ganges in great eﬅimation, for having good water near them yet they will fetch the water of Ganges a great way off, and if they have not sufficient to drink they will sprinkle a little on them and then they think themselves well[5].

From Satagam I travelled by the country of the King of Tippara or Porto Grande, with whom the Mogores or Mogen have almost continual wars. The Mogen, which be of the kingdom of Recon and Rame, be stronger than the King of Tippara, so that Chatigan, or Porto Grande, is oftentimes under the King of Recon[1].

There is a country four days' journey from Couche or Quicheu, before mentioned, which is called Bottanter and the city Bottia (the King is called Dermain), the people whereof are very tall and strong[2]. And there are merchants which come out of China—and they say out of Muscovia or Tartary—and they come to buy musk, cambals[3], agates, silk, pepper, and saffron like the saffron of Persia.

The country is very great ; three months' journey. There are very high mountains in this country, and one of them so steep that when a man is six days' journey off it he may see it perfectly[4]. Upon these mountains are people which have ears of a span long ; if their ears be not long they call them apes. They say that when they be upon the mountains they see ships in the sea sailing to and fro, but they know not from whence they come nor whither they go.

There are merchants which come out of the East, they say, from under the sun (which is, from China), which have no beards ; and they say there it is something warm, but those which come from the other side of the mountains (which is from the North) say there it is very cold.

These Northern merchants[1] are apparelled with woollen cloth and hats, white hosen, close, and boots which be of Moscovia or Tartary. They report that in their country they have very good horses, but they be little ; some men have four, five or six hundred horses and kine. They live with milk and flesh. They cut the tails of their kine and sell them very dear[2], for they be in great request and much esteemed in those parts. The hair of them is a yard long, the rump is above a span long ; they use to hang them for bravery upon the heads of their elephants ; they be much used in Pegu and China. They buy and sell by scores upon the ground. The people be very swift on foot.

From Chatigan in Bengala I came to Bacola[3], the King whereof is a Gentile, a man very well disposed and delighteth much to shoot in a gun. His country is very great and fruitful and hath store of rice, much cotton cloth and cloth of silk. The houses be very fair and high-builded, the streets large, the people naked, except a little cloth about their waist. The women wear great store of silver hoops about their necks and arms, and their legs are ringed with silver and copper and rings made of elephants' teeth.

From Bacola I went to Serrepore[1], which standeth upon the river of Ganges ; the King is called Chondery. They be all hereabout rebels against their king Zelabdim Echebar, for here are so many rivers and islands that they flee from one to another, whereby his horsemen cannot prevail against them. Great store of cotton cloth is made here.

Sinnergan[2] is a town six leagues from Serrepore, where there is the best and finest cloth made of cotton that is in all India. The chief king of all these countries is called Isacan[3], and he is chief of all the other kings and is a great friend to all Christians. The houses here, as they be in the most part of India, are very little and covered with straw and have a few mats round about the walls and the door to keep out the tigers and the foxes. Many of the people are very rich. Here they will eat no flesh nor kill no beast ; they live of rice, milk and fruits. They go with a little cloth before them and all the rest of their bodies is naked. Great store of cotton cloth goeth from hence and much rice, wherewith they serve all India, Ceilon, Pegu, Malacca, Sumatra and many other places.

I went from Serrepore the 28th of November, 1586, for Pegu, in a small ship, or foist[4], of one Albert Caravallos ; and so passing down Ganges and passing by the Island of Sundiva[5], Porto Grande or the country of Tippara, the kingdom of Recon and Mogen, leaving them on our left side with a fair wind at North-weſt, our course was South and by Eaſt, which brought us to the bar of Negrais in Pegu. If any contrary wind had come we had thrown many of our things overboard, for we were so peſtered with people and goods that there was scant place to lie in. From Bengala to Pegu is ninety leagues[1].

We entered the bar of Negrais, which is a brave bar and hath four fathoms water where it hath leaſt. Three days after we came to Cosmin[2], which is a very pretty town and ſtandeth very pleasantly, very well furnished with all things.

The people be very tall and well-disposed ; the women white[3], round-faced, with little eyes. The houses are high-built, set upon great high poſts, and they go up to them with long ladders for fear of the tigers[4], which be very many. The country is very fruitful of all things. Here are very great figs, oranges, cocoes and other fruits. The land is very high that we fall withal[5], but after we be entered the bar it is very low and full of rivers, for they go all to and fro in boats, which they call paroes[6], and keep their houses, with wife and children, in them.

From the bar of Negrais to the city of Pegu is ten days' journey by the rivers. We went from Cosmin to Pegu in paroes, or boats, and passing up the rivers

PORTUGUESE SOLDIER TAKING HIS PLEASURE IN A PALANQUIN

[facing p. 120

we came to Medon[1], which is a pretty town where there be a wonderful number of paroes, for they keep their houses and their markets in them all upon the water. They row to and fro and have all their merchandises in their boats, with a great Sombrero[2] or shadow over their heads to keep the sun from them, which is as broad as a great cart-wheel, made of the leaves of the coco trees and fig trees and is very light.

From Medon we went to Dela[3], which is a very fair town and hath a fair port into the sea, from whence go many ships to Malacca, Mecca and many other places. Here are eighteen or twenty very great and long houses, where they tame and keep many elephants of the king's ; for thereabout in the wilderness they catch the wild elephants. It is a very fruitful country.

From Dela we went to Cirion[4], which is a good town and hath a fair port into the sea, whither come many ships from Mecca, Malacca, Sumatra, and from divers other places ; and there the ships stay and discharge, and send up their goods in paroes to Pegu.

From Cirion we went to Macao[5], which is a pretty town ; where we left our boats or paroes and in the morning taking Delingeges[6], which are a kind of coaches, made of cords and cloth quilted and carried upon a stang[7] between three or four men, we came to Pegu the same day.

Pegu is a city very great ; strong and very fair,

with walls of stone and great ditches round about it. There are two towns, the old town and the new. In the old town are all the merchants—strangers and very many merchants of the country.

All the goods are sold in the old town, which is very great and hath many suburbs round about it ; and all the houses are made of canes which they call bambos and be covered with straw. In your house you have a warehouse, which they call Godon[1], which is made of brick to put your goods in ; for oftentimes they take fire and burn in an hour four or five hundred houses, so that if the Godon were not you should be in danger to have all burned, if any wind should rise, at a trice[2].

In the new town is the king and all his nobility and gentry. It is a city very great and populous and is made square and with very fair walls, and a great ditch round about it full of water with many crocodiles in it. It hath twenty gates and they be made of stone ; for every square[3] five gates. There are also many turrets for sentinels to watch, made of wood and gilded with gold very fair.

The streets are the fairest that ever I saw, as straight as a line from one gate to the other, and so broad that ten or twelve men may ride a-front through them. On both sides of them at every man's door is set a palmer tree (which is the nut tree), which make a very fair show and a very commodious shadow, so that a man may walk in the shade all day. The houses be made of wood and covered with tiles.

The king's house is in the middle of the city and is walled and ditched round about ; and the buildings within are made of wood very sumptuously gilded, and great workmanship is upon the forefront, which is likewise very costly gilded. And the house wherein his Pagode or idol standeth, is covered with tiles of silver, and all the walls are gilded with gold.

Within the first gate of the king's house is a great large room, on both sides whereof are houses made for the king's elephants, which be marvellous great and fair and are brought up to wars and in service of the king. And among the rest he hath four white elephants, which are very strange and rare, for there is none other king which hath them but he ; if any other king hath one he will send unto him for it. When any of these white elephants is brought unto the king all the merchants in the city are commanded to see them and to give him a present of half a ducat, which doth come to a great sum, for that there are many merchants in the city. After that you have given your present you may come and see them at your pleasure, although they stand in the king's house.

This king in his title is called the King of the White Elephants. If any other king have one and will not send it him he will make war with him for it, for he had rather lose a great part of his kingdom than not to conquer him. They do very great service unto these white elephants. Every one of them standeth in an house gilded with gold, and they do feed in vessels of silver and gilt. One of them when he doth go to the river to be washed, as every day they do, goeth under a canopy of cloth of gold or of silk carried over him by six or eight men, and eight or ten men go before him playing on drums, shawmes[1] or other instruments ; and when he is washed and cometh out of the river there is a gentleman which doth wash his feet in a silver basin, which is his office given him by the king.

There is no such account made of any black elephant, be he never so great—and surely there be wonderful fair and great, and some be nine cubits[2] in height. And they do report that the king hath above five thousand elephants of war, besides many other which be not taught to fight.

This king hath a very large place wherein he taketh the wild elephants. It standeth about a mile from Pegu, builded with a fair court within, and is in a great grove or wood. And there be many huntsmen which go into the wilderness with she-elephants, for without the she they are not to be taken. And they be taught for that purpose and every hunter hath five or six of them ; and they say that they anoint the she-elephants with a certain ointment, which when the wild elephant doth smell he will not leave her. When they have brought the wild elephant near unto the place they send word unto the town, and many horsemen and footmen come out and cause the she-elephant to enter into a strait way which doth go to the palace[1], and the she and he do run in (for it is like a wood) and when they be in the gate doth shut. Afterward they get out the female, and when the male seeth that he is left alone he weepeth and crieth and runneth against the walls, which be made of so strong trees that some of them do break their teeth with running against them[2]. Then they prick him with sharp canes and cause him to go into a strait house, and there they put a rope about his middle and about his feet and let him stand there three or four days without eating or drinking, and then they bring a female to him, with meat and drink, and within few days he becometh tame.

The chief force of the king is in these elephants, and when they go into the wars they set a frame of wood upon their backs, bound with great cords, wherein sit four or six men, which fight with guns, bows and arrows, darts, and other weapons. And they say that their skins are so thick that a pellet of an harquebus will scarce pierce them, except it be in some tender place. Their weapons be very bad. They have guns, but shoot very badly in them ; darts and swords, short without points[1].

The king keepeth a very great state. When he sitteth abroad, as he doth every day twice, all his noblemen (which they call Shemines[2]) sit on each side, a good distance off, and a great guard without them. The courtyard is very great. If any man will speak with the king he is to kneel down, to heave up his hands to his head, and to put his head to the ground three times—when he entereth, in the middle way, and when he cometh near to the king ; and then he sitteth down and talketh with the king. If the king like well of him he sitteth near him within three or four paces ; if he think not well of him he sitteth further off.

When he goeth to war he goeth very strong. At my being there he went to Odia[3], in the country of Siam, with three hundred thousand men and five thousand elephants. Thirty thousand men were his guard.

These people do eat roots, herbs, leaves, dogs, cats, rats, serpents and snakes ; they refuse almost nothing.

When the king rideth abroad he rideth with a great guard and many noblemen ; oftentimes upon an elephant with a fine castle upon him very fairly gilded with gold, and sometimes upon a great frame like an horse-litter, which hath a little house upon it covered overhead but open on the sides, which is all gilded with gold and set with many rubies and sapphires (whereof he hath infinite store in his country), and is carried upon sixteen or eighteen men's shoulders. This coach in their language is called Serrion. Very great feasting and triumphing is many times before the king, both of men and women.

This king hath little force by sea, because he hath but very few ships. He hath houses full of gold and silver and bringeth in often but spendeth very little, and hath the mines of rubies and sapphires and spinels. Near unto the palace of the king there is a treasure wonderful rich, the which, because it is so near, he doth not account of it, and it standeth open for all men to see in a great walled court with two gates, which be always open. There are four houses gilded very richly and covered with lead; in every one of them are Pagodes or images of huge stature and great value. In the first is the picture[1] of a king in gold, with a crown of gold on his head full of great rubies and sapphires, and about him there stand four children of gold. In the second house is the picture of a man in silver wonderful great, as high as an house; his foot is as long as a man and he is made sitting, with a crown on his head very rich with stones. In the third house is the picture of a man greater than the other, made of brass, with a rich crown on his head. In the fourth and last house doth stand another, made of brass, greater than the other, with a crown also on his head very rich with stones.

In another court not far from this stand four other Pagodes or idols marvellous great, of copper, made in the same place where they do stand ; for they be so great that they be not to be removed. They stand in four houses fair, and are themselves gilded all over, save their heads, and they show like a black Morian[1]. Their expenses in gilding of their images are wonderful.

The king hath one wife and above three hundred concubines, by which they say he hath fourscore or fourscore and ten children. He sitteth in judgment almost every day. They use no speech, but give up their supplications written in the leaves of a tree with the point of an iron bigger than a bodkin[2]. These leaves are an ell long and about two inches broad ; they are also double. He which giveth in his supplication doth stand in a place a little distance off, with a present. If his matter be liked of, the king accepteth of his present and granteth his request ; if his suit be not liked of, he returneth with his present, for the king will not take it.

In India there are few commodities which serve for Pegu, except opium of Cambaia, painted cloth of San Thomé[3] or of Masulipatan, and white cloth of

Bengala, which is spent[1] there in great quantity. They bring thither also much cotton-yarn, red-coloured with a root which they called Saia[2], which will never lose his colour ; it is very well sold here and very much of it cometh yearly to Pegu. By your money you lose much[3].

The ships which come from Bengala, San Thomé and Masulipatan come to the bar of Negrais and to Cosmin. To Martavan[4]—a port of the sea in the kingdom of Pegu—come many ships laden with Sandal, Porcelains and other wares of China, and with Camphora of Borneo and pepper from Achen in Sumatra. To Cirion—a port of Pegu—come ships from Mecca with woollen cloth, Scarlets, velvets, opium and suchlike.

There are in Pegu eight Brokers, whom they call Tareghe[5], which are bound to sell your goods at the price which they be worth, and you give them for their labour two in the hundred ; and they be bound to make your debt good, because you sell your merchandises upon their word. If the broker pay you not at his day you may take him home and keep him in your house ; which is a great shame for him. And if he pay you not presently, you may take his wife and children and his slaves and bind them at your door and set them in the Sun, for that is the law of the country.

Their current money in these parts is a kind of brass, which they call Gansa[1], wherewith you may buy gold, silver, rubies, musk and all other things. The gold and silver is merchandise, and is worth sometimes more and sometimes less, as other wares be. This brazen money doth go by a weight which they call a biza,[2] and commonly this biza, after our account, is worth about half-a-crown, or somewhat less.

The merchandise[3] which be in Pegu are gold, silver, rubies, sapphires, spinels, musk, benjamin[4] or frankincense, long pepper, tin, lead, copper, lacca[5] (whereof they make hard wax), rice and wine made of rice[6], and some sugar. The elephants do eat the sugar-canes, or else they would make very much. And they consume many canes likewise in making of their Varellaes[7], or Idol temples, which are in great numbers, both great and small. They be made round like a sugar-loaf; some are as high as a Church, very broad beneath, some a quarter of a mile in compass. Within they be all earth done about with stone.

They consume in these Varellaes great quantities of gold; for that they be all gilded aloft, and many of them from the top to the bottom. And every ten or twelve years they must be new gilded, because the rain consumeth off the gold, for they stand open abroad. If they did not consume their gold in these vanities it would be very plentiful and good cheap in Pegu.

About two days' journey from Pegu there is a Varelle or Pagode which is the pilgrimage of the Pegues. It is called Dogonne[1], and is of a wonderful bigness and all gilded from the foot to the top. And there is an house by it wherein the Tallipoies[2], which are their Priests, do preach. This house is five and fifty paces in length, and hath three pawns[3] or walks in it and forty great pillars, gilded, which stand between the walks ; and it is open on all sides with a number of small pillars, which be likewise gilded. It is gilded with gold within and without.

There are houses very fair round about for the pilgrims to lie in, and many goodly houses for the Tallipoies to preach in, which are full of images, both of men and women, which are all gilded over with gold. It is the fairest place, as I suppose, that is in the world. It standeth very high and there are four ways to it, which all along are set with trees of fruits, in such wise that a man may go in the shade above two miles in length. And when their feast day is, a man can hardly pass by water or by land for the great press of people, for they come from all places of the kingdom of Pegu thither at their feast.

In Pegu they have many Tallipoies or priests, which preach against all abuses. Many men resort unto them. When they enter into their Kiack[1] (that is to say, their holy place or temple) at the door there is a great jar of water with a cock or a ladle in it, and there they wash their feet, and then they enter in and lift up their hands to their heads, first to their preacher and then to the Sun, and so sit down.

The Tallipoies go very strangely apparelled, with one camboline, or thin cloth, next to their body of a brown colour, another of yellow, doubled many times, upon their shoulder, and those two be girded to them with a broad girdle. And they have a skin of leather hanging on a string about their necks, whereupon they sit, bareheaded and barefooted (for none of them weareth shoes), with their right arms bare[2] and a great broad sombrero or shadow in their hands to defend them in the Summer from the Sun and in the Winter from the rain.

When the Tallipoies or priests take their Orders, first they go to school until they be twenty years old or more, and then they come before a Tallipoie appointed for that purpose, whom they call Rowli[3]; he is of the chiefest and most learned, and he opposeth them and afterward examineth them many times, whether they will leave their friends and the company of all women and take upon them the habit of a Tallipoie. If any be content, then he rideth upon an horse about the streets, very richly apparelled, with drums and pipes ; to show that he leaveth the riches of the world to be a Tallipoie. In few days after he is carried upon a thing like an horse-litter (which they call a Serion) upon ten or twelve men's shoulders, in the apparel of a Tallipoie, with pipes and drums, and many Tallipoies with him and all his friends, and so they go with him to his house, which standeth without the town, and there they leave him.

Every one of them hath his house, which is very little, set upon six or eight posts, and they go up to them with a ladder of twelve or fourteen staves[1]. Their houses be for the most part by the highway's side and among the trees and in the woods.

And they go with a great pot, made of wood or fine earth and covered, tied with a broad girdle upon their shoulder which cometh under their arm ; wherewith they go to beg their victuals which they eat[2], which is rice, fish and herbs. They demand nothing, but come to the door, and the people presently do give them some one thing and some another, and they put all together in their pot ; for they say they must eat of their alms and therewith content themselves.

They keep their feasts by the Moon, and when it is new Moon they keep their greatest feast ; and then the people send rice and other things to that Kiack or Church of which they be, and there all the Tallipoies do meet which be of that Church and eat the victuals which are sent them. When the Tallipoies do preach many of the people carry them gifts into the pulpit where they sit and preach, and there is one that sitteth by them to take that which the people bring; it is divided among them. They have none other ceremonies nor service that I could see, but only preaching.

I went from Pegu to Jamahey, which is in the country of the Langeiannes, whom we call Jangomes[1]; it is five and twenty days' journey North-east from Pegu. In which journey I passed many fruitful and pleasant countries. The country is very low and hath many fair rivers. The houses are very bad, made of canes and covered with straw. Here are many wild buffes and elephants.

Jamahey is a very fair and great town, with fair houses of stone, well peopled; the streets are very large. The men very well set and strong, with a cloth about them, bare-headed and bare-footed, for in all these countries they wear no shoes. The women be much fairer than those of Pegu[2].

Here in all these countries they have no wheat; they make some cakes of rice. Hither to Jamahey come many merchants out of China and bring great store of musk, gold, silver and many other things of China work. Here is great store of victuals; they have such plenty that they will not milk the buffles, as they do in all other places. Here is great store of copper and benjamin.

In these countries, when the people be sick they make a vow to offer meat[1] unto the devil if they escape; and when they be recovered they make a banquet, with many pipes and drums and other instruments, and dancing all the night; and their friends come and bring gifts, cocoes, figs, arrecaes[2] and other fruits, and with great dancing and rejoicing they offer to the devil, and say they give the devil to eat and drive him out. When they be dancing and playing they will cry and halloa very loud, and in this sort they say they drive him away. And when they be sick a Tallipoie or two every night doth sit by them and sing, to please the devil that he should not hurt them. And if any die he is carried upon a great frame made like a tower, with a covering all gilded with gold made of canes, carried with fourteen or sixteen men, with drums and pipes and other instruments playing before him, to a place out of the town and there is burned. He is accompanied with all his friends and neighbours, all men, and they give to the Tallipoies, or priests, many mats and cloth. And then they return to the house and there make a feast for two days, and then the wife, with all the neighbours' wives and her friends, go to the place where he was burned and there they sit a certain time and cry, and gather the pieces of bones which be left unburned and bury them, and then return to their houses and make an end of all mourning. And the men and women which be near of kin do shave their heads ; which they do not use except it be for the death of a friend, for they much esteem of their hair.

Caplan[1] is the place where they find the rubies, sapphires and spinels[2] it standeth six days' journey from Ava in the kingdom of Pegu. There are many great high hills out of which they dig them. None may go to the pits but only those which dig them.

In Pegu, and in all the countries of Ava[3], Langeiannes, Siam and the Bramas[4], the men wear bunches or little round balls in their privy members ; some of them wear two and some three. They cut the skin and so put them in, one into one side and another into the other side, which they do when they be twenty-five or thirty years old, and at their pleasure they take one or more of them out as they think good. When they be married, the husband is (for every child which his wife hath) to put in one until he come to three and then no more ; for they say the women do desire them. They were invented because they should not abuse the male sex, for in times past all those countries were so given to that villainy that they were very scarce of people[5].

It was also ordained that the women should not

have paſt three cubits[1] of cloth in their nether clothes which they bind about them ; which are so ſtrait that when they go in the ſtreets they show one side of the leg bare above the knee.

The bunches aforesaid be of divers sorts ; the leaſt be as big as a little walnut and very round, the greateſt are as big as a little hen's egg. Some are of brass and some of silver, but those of silver be for the king and his noblemen ; these are gilded and made with great cunning and ring like a little bell. There are some made of lead, which they call Selwy, because they ring but little, and these be of lesser price for the poorer sort. The king sometimes taketh his out and giveth them to his noblemen as a great gift, and because he hath used them they eſteem them greatly. They will put one in and heal up the place in seven or eight days.

The Bramas which be of the king's country (for the king is a Brama) have their legs or bellies or some part of their body, as they think good themselves, made black with certain things which they have. They use to prick the skin and to put on it a kind of anile or blacking, which doth continue always[2]. And this is counted an honour among them, but none may have it but the Bramas which are of the king's kindred.

These people wear no beards ; they pull out the hair or their faces with little pinsons[3] made for that purpose. Some of them will let sixteen or twenty hairs grow together, some in one place of his face and some in another, and pulleth out all the rest ; for he carrieth his pinsons always with him to pull the hairs out as soon as they appear. If they see a man with a beard they wonder at him. They have their teeth blacked, both men and women, for they say a dog hath his teeth white, therefore they will black theirs[1].

The Pegues, if they have a suit in the law which is so doubtful that they cannot well determine it, put two long canes into the water where it is very deep, and both the parties go into the water by the poles, and there sit men to judge ; and they both do dive under the water and he which remaineth longest under the water doth win the suit.

The 10th of January I went from Pegu to Malacca, passing by many of the ports of Pegu, as Martavan, the Island of Tavi (from whence cometh great store of tin which serveth all India), the Islands of Tanaseri, Junsalaon[2], and many others, and so came to Malacca the 8th of February, where the Portugals have a castle which standeth near the sea.

And the country fast[3] without the town belongeth to the Malayos, which is a kind of proud people. They go naked with a cloth about their middle and a little roll of cloth about their heads.

Hither come many ships from China and from the

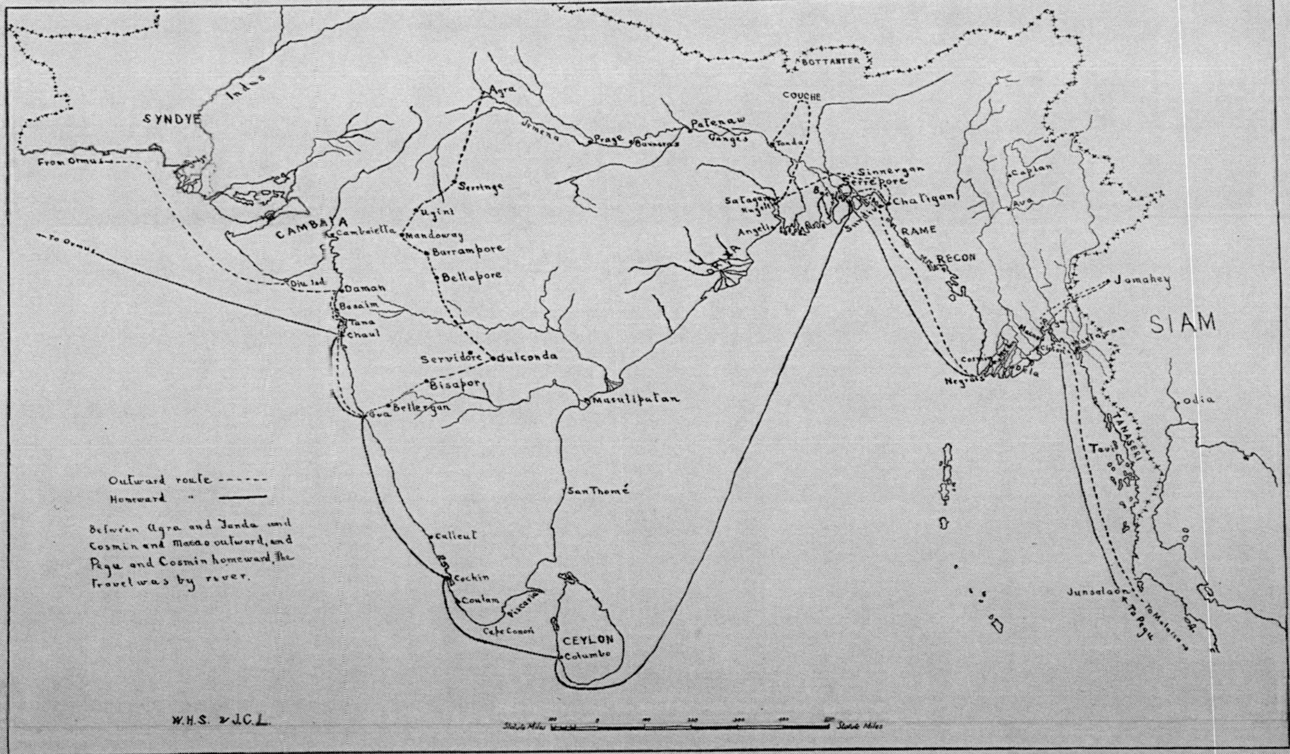

FITCH'S INDIAN VOYAGES AND JOURNEYS

[facing p. 158

Malucos[1], Banda, Timor, and from many other Islands of the Javas, which bring great store of spices and drugs and diamonds and other jewels. The voyages into many of these Islands belong unto the Captain of Malacca[2] (so that none may go thither without his licence), which yield him great sums of money every year.

The Portugals here have oftentimes wars with the king of Achem[3], which standeth in the Island of Sumatra ; from whence cometh great store of pepper and other spices every year to Pegu and Mecca within the Red Sea and other places.

When the Portugals go from Macao[4], in China, to Japan, they carry much white silk, gold, musk and porcelains ; and they bring from thence nothing but silver. They have a great carack[5] which goeth thither every year, and she bringeth from thence every year above six hundred thousand crusadoes[6] ; and all this silver of Japan, and two hundred thousand crusadoes more in silver which they bring yearly out of India, they employ to their great advantage in China, and they bring from thence gold, musk, silk, copper, porcelains and many other things very costly and gilded.

When the Portugals come to Canton in China to traffic they must remain there but certain days ; and when they come in at the gate of the city they must enter their names in a book, and when they go out at night they must put out their names. They may not lie in the town all night, but must lie in their boats without the town. And their days being expired, if any man remain there they are evil used and imprisoned. The Chinians are very suspicious and do not trust strangers ; it is thought that the king doth not know that any strangers come into his country.

And, further, it is credibly reported that the common people see their king very seldom or not at all, nor may not look up to that place where he sitteth. And when he rideth abroad he is carried upon a great chair or serrion gilded very fair, wherein there is made a little house with a lattice to look out at, so that he may see them but they may not look up at him[1]. And all the time that he passeth by them they heave up their hands to their heads and lay their heads on the ground, and look not up until he be passed.

The order of China is, when they mourn, that they wear white thread shoes[2] and hats of straw. The man doth mourn for his wife two years, the wife for her husband three years, the son for his father a year and for his mother two years. And all the time which they mourn they keep the dead in the house, the bowels being taken out and filled with chownam[3] or lime, and coffined ; and when the time is expired they carry them out, playing and piping, and burn them. And when they return they pull off their mourning weeds and marry at their pleasure. A man may keep as many concubines as he will, but one wife only. All the Chineans, Japonians and Cauchin-Chineans do write right downwards, and they do write with a fine pencil made of dogs' or cats' hair[1].

Laban is an Island among the Javas, from whence come the diamonds of the new water ; and they find them in the rivers, for the king will not suffer them to dig the rock.

Jamba is an Island among the Javas[2], also, from whence come diamonds. And the King hath a mass of earth which is gold ; it groweth in the middle of a river. And when the King doth lack gold they cut part of the earth and melt it, whereof cometh gold. This mass of earth doth appear but once in a year, which is when the water is low ; and this is in the month of April.

Bima is another Island among the Javas, where the women travail and labour as our men do in England, and the men keep house and go where they will[3].

The 29th of March, 1588, I returned from Malacca to Martavan and so to Pegu, where I remained the second time until the 17th of September, and then I went to Cosmin and there took shipping ; and, passing many dangers by reason of contrary winds, it pleased God that we arrived in Bengala in November following, where I stayed for want of passage until the 3rd of February, 1589, and then I shipped myself for Cochin. In which voyage we endured great extremity for lack of fresh water; for the weather was extreme hot and we were many merchants and passengers, and we had very many calms and hot weather. Yet it pleased God that we arrived in Ceylon the 6th of March, where we stayed five days to water and to furnish ourselves with other necessary provision.

This Ceylon is a brave Island, very fruitful and fair, but by reason of continual wars with the king thereof all things are very dear; for he will not suffer anything to be brought to the castle where the Portugals be, wherefore oftentimes they have great want of victuals. Their provision of victuals cometh out of Bengala every year.

The King is called Raia[1] and is of great force, for he cometh to Columbo—which is the place where the Portugals have their fort—with an hundred thousand men and many elephants. But they be naked[2] people all of them, yet many of them be good with their pieces, which be muskets.

When the king talketh with any man he standeth upon one leg and setteth the other foot upon his knee[3] with his sword in his hand; it is not their order for the King to sit but to stand. His apparel is a fine painted cloth made of cotton-wool about his middle ; his hair is long and bound up with a little fine cloth about his head ; all the rest of his body is naked. His guard are a thousand men, which stand round about him and he in the middle, and when he marcheth many of them go before him and the rest come after him.

They are of the race of the Chingalayes[1], which they say are the best kind of all the Malabars. Their ears are very large, for the greater they are the more honourable they are accounted ; some of them are a span long. The wood which they burn is Cinamom wood, and it smelleth very sweet. There is great store of rubies, sapphires and spinels in this Island ; the best kind of all be here, but the king will not suffer the inhabitants to dig for them lest his enemies should know of them and make wars against him, and so drive him out of his country for them.

They have no horses in all the country. The elephants be not so great as those of Pegu, which be monstrous huge, but they say all other elephants do fear them and none dare fight with them, though they be very small.

Their women have a cloth bound about them from their middle to their knee and all the rest is bare. All of them be black and but little, both men and women. Their houses are very little, made of the branches of the palmer, or coco-tree, and covered with the leaves of the same tree.

The 11th of March we sailed from Ceylon and so doubled the cape of Comori[1]. Not far from thence, between Ceylon and the mainland of Negapatan[2], they fish for pearls. And there is fished every year very much, which doth serve all India, Cambaia and Bengala ; it is not so orient as the pearl of Baharim in the Gulf of Persia.

From Cape de Comori we passed by Coulam[3], which is a fort of the Portugals. From whence cometh great store of pepper, which cometh for Portugal ; for oftentimes there ladeth one of the caracks of Portugal.

Thus passing the coast we arrived in Cochin the 22nd of March, where we found the weather warm, but scarcity of victuals ; for here groweth neither corn nor rice and the greatest part cometh from Bengala.

They have here very bad water, for the river is far off. This bad water causeth many of the people to be like lepers, and many of them have their legs swollen as big as a man in the waist[4], and many of them are scant able to go.

These people here be Malabars and of the race of the Naires[5] of Calicut, and they differ much from the other Malabars. These have their heads very full of hair and bound up with a string; and there doth appear a bush without the band wherewith it is bound. The men be tall and strong and good archers with a long-bow and a long arrow, which is their best weapon; yet there be some calivers[1] among them, but they handle them badly.

Here groweth the pepper, and it springeth up by a tree or a pole and is like our ivy-berry, but something longer, like the wheat-ear. And at first the bunches are green, and as they wax ripe they cut them off and dry them. The leaf is much lesser than the ivy-leaf and thinner.

All the inhabitants here have very little houses covered with the leaves of the coco-trees. The men be of a reasonable stature, the women little; all black, with a cloth bound about their middle hanging down to their hams; all the rest of their bodies are naked. They have horrible great ears with many rings set with pearls and stones in them.

The king goeth incached[2], as they do all. He doth not remain in a place above five or six days; he hath many houses, but they be but little. His guard is but small. He removeth from one house to another according to their order[3].

All the pepper of Calicut and coarse cinamom groweth here in this country. The best cinamom doth come from Ceylon, and is pilled[4] from fine young trees.

Here are very many palmer or coco trees, which is their chief food ; for it is their meat and drink and yieldeth many other necessary things, as I have declared before.

The Nairs which be under the king of Samorin[1], which be Malabars, have always wars with the Portugals. The king hath always peace with them; but his people go to the sea to rob and steal. Their chief captain is called Cogi Alli[2] ; he hath three castles under him. When the Portugals complain to the king he saith he doth not send them out ; but he consenteth that they go. They range all the coast from Ceylon to Goa, and go by four or five parowes or boats together, and have in every one of them fifty or threescore men, and board presently[3]. They do much harm on that coast and take every year many foists and boats of the Portugals. Many of these people be Moors. This king's country beginneth twelve leagues from Cochin and reacheth near unto Goa.

I remained in Cochin until the 2nd of November, which was eight months, for that there was no passage that went away in all that time ; if I had come two days sooner I had found a passage presently. From Cochin I went to Goa, where I remained three days ; from Cochin to Goa is an hundred leagues[4]. From Goa I went to Chaul, which is threescore leagues[5], where I remained three and twenty days. And there making my provision of things necessary for the ship, from thence I departed to Ormus, where I stayed for a passage to Balsara fifty days ; from Goa to Ormus is four hundred leagues.

Here I thought good, before I make an end of this my book, to declare some things which India and the country farther Eastward do bring forth.

The pepper groweth in many parts of India, especially about Cochin, and much of it doth grow in the fields among the bushes without any labour, and when it is ripe they go and gather it. The shrub is like unto our ivy tree, and if it did not run about some tree or pole it would fall down and rot. When they first gather it it is green, and then they lay it in the Sun and it becometh black.

The ginger groweth like unto our garlic[1], and the root is the ginger ; it is to be found in many parts of India.

The cloves do come from the Isles of the Moluccoes, which be divers Islands ; their tree is like to our bay tree.

The nutmegs and maces grow together and come from the Isle of Banda ; the tree is like to our walnut tree, but somewhat lesser.

The white sandal is wood very sweet and in great request among the Indians, for they grind it with a little water and anoint their bodies therewith ; it cometh from the Isle of Timor[2].

Camphora is a precious thing among the Indians and is sold dearer than gold. I think none of it cometh for Christendom. That which is compounded cometh from China, but that which groweth in canes and is the best cometh from the great Isle of Borneo[1].

Lignum Aloes[2] cometh from Cauchinchina.

The benjamin cometh out of the countries of Siam and Jangomes.

The long pepper groweth in Bengala, in Pegu and in the Islands of the Javas.

The musk cometh out of Tartary and is made after this order, by report of the merchants which bring it to Pegu to sell. In Tartary there is a little beast like unto a young roe, which they take in snares and beat him to death with the blood. After that they cut out the bones and beat the flesh with the blood very small and fill the skin with it; and hereof cometh the musk[3].

Of the amber they hold divers opinions; but most men say it cometh out of the sea, and that they find it upon the shore's side.

The rubies, sapphires and spinels are found in Pegu.

The diamonds are found in divers places, as in Bisnagar[4], in Agra, in Delli and in the Islands of the Javas.

The best pearls come from the Island of Baharim in the Persian sea; the worser from the Piscaria[5] near

THE PEARL-FISHERY AT TUTICORIN

[facing p. 148

the Isle of Ceylon and from Aynam[1], a great Island on the Southermost coast of China.

Spodium[2] and many other kinds of drugs come from Cambaia.

Now to return to my voyage. From Ormus I went to Balsara or Basora and from Basora to Babylon ; and we passed the most part of the way by the strength of men, by hauling the boat up the river with a long cord. From Babylon I came by land to Mosul (which standeth near to Ninive, which is all ruinated and destroyed) ; it standeth fast by the river of Tigris. From Mosul I went to Merdin[3], which is in the country of the Armenians, but now there dwell in that place a people which they call Cordies or Curdi[4].

From Merdin I went to Orfa, which is a very fair town (and it hath a goodly fountain full of fish), where the Moors hold many great ceremonies and opinions concerning Abraham ; for they say he did once dwell there[5]. From thence I went to Bir and so passed the river of Euphrates[6].

From Bir I went to Aleppo, where I stayed certain months for company, and then I went to Tripolis, where finding English shipping I came with a prosperous voyage to London, where by God's assistance I safely arrived the 29th of April, 1591, having been eight years out of my native country.

And so endeth the Relation of Master Ralph Fitch.

Here is added, to conclude and for more enlightenment, a brief Relation of the great magnificence and rich traffic of the Kingdom of Pegu beyond the East India; written by Frey Peter of Lisbon to his cousin Frey Diego of Lisbon, from Cochin, the 28th December, 1589.

I received your letters in the harbour of Damaon[1] by a caravel[2] of advice that came from Malacca; which brought shot, powder and other provision for the furnishing of four galleys and a great galleon, which are now in building to keep our coast for fear of great store of men of war, being Moors, which trouble us very sore.

At that instant when I received your letters I was newly come from the kingdom of Pegu, where I had remained one year and an half; and from thence I departed to the city of Cochin in October, 1587. The news which I can certify you of concerning these countries are that this King of Pegu is the mightiest king of men, and the richest that is in these parts of the world. For he bringeth into the field, at any time when he hath wars with other Princes, above a million of fighting men; howbeit they be very lean and small people and are brought unto the field without good order.

He is lord of the Elephants, and of all the gold and silver mines, and of all the pearls and precious stones; so that he hath the greatest store of treasure that ever was heard of in these parts. The country people call him The God of Truth and of Justice.

I had great conference with this King and with the head Captain of the Portugals, which is one of the country. They demanded of me many questions as touching the law and faith of Jesus Christ and as touching the Ten Commandments. And the King gave his consent that our Order should build a church in his country, which was half builded, but our perverse and malicious Portugals plucked it down again.

For whereas it is a country wherein our nation gain very much by their commodities, they fearing that by the building of this church there would be greater resort thither, and so their trade should be impaired if their great gains should be known unto others than those which found this country out first, therefore they were so unwilling that the building of this church should go forward. Our Portugals which are here in this realm are worse people than the Gentiles.

I preached divers times among those heathen people ; but, being obstinate, they say that as their fathers believed so they will believe, for if their forefathers went to the devil so they will. Whereupon I returned back again to our monastery to certify our Father Provincial of the estate of this new-found country. It is the best and richest country in all this East India, and it is thought to be richer than China.

I am afraid that the wars which His Majesty hath with England will be the utter undoing and spoil[1] of Spain; for these countries likewise are almost spoiled with civil wars, which the Moors have against the Gentiles; for the kings here are up in arms all the country over.

Here is an Indian which is counted a Prophet, which hath prophesied that there will a Dragon arise in a strange country which will do great hurt to Spain. How it will fall out, only God doth know. And thus I rest, from this monastery of Cochin, the 28th of December, 1589.

Your good cousin and assured friend,

Friar Peter of Lisbon.

Which endeth the whole.

NOTES

[1] *Page* 19. Thomas Stevens was born at Bourton, in Dorset, apparently about 1549; became a scholar of Winchester in 1564; was for a time, says Hakluyt, at New College, Oxford; went to Rome and was admitted to the Society of Jesus in 1575; sailed to Goa as he tells us and did missionary work there for forty years. He was the first to study Canarese scientifically and published grammars of that and Hindustani, as well as books of religious instruction in both tongues. He died at Goa in 1619.

[2] *Page* 19. Inform.

[3] *Page* 19. Condition, state.

[4] *Page* 19. Sum up.

[5] *Page* 19. Stevens, as we know, was a Jesuit. Himself a fine soldier, Ignatius Loyola founded the "Company of Jesus" on the model of a regiment drilled and disciplined with exacting severity for its special work. Unquestioning obedience to orders was the guiding rule of Jesuits of the rank and file, and it is this "Obedience" that Stevens emphasises. It is to the credit of the Jesuits as a body that they always were obedient, at no matter what extremity of cost; hence, partly, their remarkable success as missionaries.

[6] *Page* 19. He was one of a body of Jesuits travelling to Lisbon together, and others had been appointed to go in their place; not "ordained" in the ecclesiastical sense.

[1] *Page* 20. Madera is a common spelling of the time and in Hakluyt almost invariable, but our Madeira is the true Portuguese form—probably from the Latin *materia*, "timber", because the island was so thickly wooded. Porto Santo is the smaller island forty miles or so north-easterly of Madeira.

NOTES

[1] *Page* 21. The Burning Zone answers to our Torrid Zone or Tropics, and was one of the "Climates" into which geographers, beginning with the Greeks, had traditionally divided the world. Tradition also said that within the Burning Zone the sea boiled and the land was a seared waste; it remained for the Portuguese, cautiously pushing down the west coast of Africa, to show finally that there was no such deadly Zone, but the name lingered as a reminder of the fears they overcame. The Equinoctial is our equator, and was in earlier use than that word.

[2] *Page* 21. Unclean receptacles and the ordinary processes of putrefaction produced the "worms", not any special quality in the rain-water.

[3] *Page* 21. Or Guinea Ship, or Portuguese man-o'-war; sailors still use all three names. It is a Medusa or jelly fish, *Physalia Pelagica*; one of the Order *Siphonophora*, sub-Order *Cystophorida*. It is remarkable for great size, brilliant colours and terrible stinging powers. The "strings" are the prey-capturing tentacles bearing the stinging organs which make it so "poisonous"; they do not operate as ballast. Stevens' description is otherwise exact.

[4] *Page* 21. That is, the Cape of Good Hope.

[1] *Page* 22. To "maine" a sail was to lower it. It had another form, "amain"; and to "strike amain" was to lower a topsail in salute. "Hoise" is much earlier and commoner than our present "hoist" and, as the word comes from the Old Dutch "hyssen", more correct. The seaman's elision of the vowel in "it"—inevitable in such frequent and urgent orders as, for instance, "Yarely now, hoise 't away!" accounts for the attached "t". This was a very common elision even in literary usage, witness Suckling's "Will, when speaking well won't win her, Saying nothing do 't?"; we still have our "'twas" as a result of it.

[2] *Page* 22. Shortest, nearest. The common meaning in earlier English; our present usage is later.

NOTES

[3] *Page* 22. He probably means the extreme tip of Africa, Cape Agulhas. Even that is not quite 35° South, while the Cape of Good Hope is barely 34°.

[1] *Page* 23. He describes the current methods of navigation generally, and in particular of dead-reckoning, which consisted in estimating the length and direction of your day's run according to the observed speed of the ship and her course by compass-bearing, allowing as well as you could for drift and lee-way. Until the days of the chronometer it was the mariner's only means of "guessing"—Stevens has the right word—at your longitude; and as even the log was not invented till somewhere round 1620 and you took your speed by throwing a chip or some such light matter overboard at a certain point in the bows and noting how long it took to drift to another certain point further aft; as the existence of currents was mostly imperfectly ascertained and their speed and set scarcely at all, and as the crank ships made almost as much lee-way as head-way on most points of sailing, it was a lucky dead-reckoning that gave you a land-fall within a day or a hundred miles of your calculations. Small wonder that the early navigators watched every sea-beast, every bird, every scrap of floating weed. To us it seems that they must have smelt their way from land to land.

[2] *Page* 23. True North.

[3] *Page* 23. It is curious that this spelling of "swerve" should have persisted in literature even into the nineteenth century; Scott was one of the latest to use it. The existence of other words in wide-spread dialect use, properly spelt so, but with different meanings, may explain the tenacity.

[4] *Page* 23. Here the "Point" seems to be the whole southern extremity of Africa generally, neither specifically the Cape of Good Hope nor Cape Agulhas.

[5] *Page* 23. A curious way of expressing it, but a quarter-point is a sub-division of the compass-card equal to 2° 48′ 45″

of the circle, and he means that the variation was round about 30° to 40° East.

[6] *Page* 23. So far as the history of magnetic variation goes all this seems dangerously inaccurate. It is not likely that the line of no-variation passed through the Azores in 1579 or anywhere near them ; nor are the other phenomena less dubious ; though it is just possible that in the neighbourhood of the Cape of Good Hope the needle would show true North or thereabouts at that time. Making Socotra instead of India is no surprising result of such uncertain knowledge.

[7] *Page* 23. "Coast" suggests itself, but it is "people" in the original Hakluyt.

[8] *Page* 23. The Wandering Albatross or Cape Sheep ; though, as it is generally nearer ten feet in span than five, possibly one of the other Albatrosses may be meant.

[1] *Page* 24. Nothing is lacking to them.

[2] *Page* 24. Peculiarity ; characteristic property. "Propriety" was at first only a variant spelling of "property", and down to the late seventeenth century was used in cases where we should use "property" exclusively. We have the sense still in "to appropriate" a thing.

[3] *Page* 24. To bow—pronounced as in "fiddle-bow"—is to bend. We retain the elbow-bending sense still in "akimbo". The Rushtail is the Tropic Bird or Bo'sun Bird, *Phaethon* ; the Forked Tail may be a Frigate Bird, Skua or Tern ; the Velvet sleeves—the Portuguese name is *Mangas de Velludo*—is the sea-mew, *Larus canus*, white with black wings.

[4] *Page* 24. The Portuguese *tubarão* or *tuberão*, "shark" and much earlier and commoner than "shark", at least in written English. It was also spelt "tiburon", "tiberune" and otherwise.

[5] *Page* 24. Here, as often formerly, a "garde" is a coloured band or stripe.

NOTES

[1] *Page* 25. The Pilot-Fish, *Naucrates ductor*. It is said to lead the shark to food, and, in return, to find abundant food for itself in what is excreted by the shark. The terror of its companion does, at any rate, afford it complete protection. It is one of the Horse-Mackerel tribe, so the description of markings is exact.

[2] *Page* 25. The Sucking-Fish, *Remora brachyptera*, does attach itself to sharks; its medicinal functions, however, have not yet been investigated.

[3] *Page* 25. That is, of the Sharks.

[4] *Page* 25. May be a Tunny or Bonito; they and other fish are indifferently called Albacore—our present spelling.

[1] *Page* 26. The Flying-Fish has fins, apart from those he glides with. The impulse for the glide probably is given by the very powerful tail. The Albacore would have little chance of keeping up with the first five hundred feet of his flight; he might then be going twenty miles an hour. The Sea-Crow I have not identified.

[2] *Page* 26. The "Point" is here once more the Cape of Good Hope—"so feared of all men" because of its storms. When Bartolomeo Diaz, the Portuguese, discovered it in 1486, he named it Cabo Tormentoso, that is, "Cape Tempestuous".

[3] *Page* 26. Mistaken, deceived. This sense continued till late in the nineteenth century—perhaps still continues in dialect.

[4] *Page* 26. Solid, with a slight sense of hard-tempered.

[5] *Page* 26. These may have been lions and were certainly not tigers; the names are constantly interchanged by early travellers, who had no anxiety for first-hand knowledge on the subject, and lions were very numerous then in the Cape Province. It is quite probable, however, that leopards or cheetahs are meant, both plentiful behind all those coasts then and both still called "tiger" by the Dutch.

[1] *Page* 27. Madagascar. Called the Isle of St. Laurence because the first European to see it—Diego Diaz, captain of

an India-bound Portuguese ship—sighted it upon the Feast of St. Laurence, 10th of August, 1500. It held the name on maps and charts for a century.

[2] *Page* 27. With anxiety and distress; we have the sense still in such phrases as "a heavy heart".

[1] *Page* 28. He describes scurvy with sufficient exactness, though he might have added more horrors without exceeding the truth. Until the days of Captain Cook it remained the dread pest of all long-voyage sailors, and indeed for long after until his wise dietetic reforms became general. By "fluxes" he probably means dysentery, for which flux was an early name, but it might have been one of many other kinds of illness with related symptoms, all having some kind of "flowing" in common.

[2] *Page* 28. These India ships from Lisbon commonly carried somewhere round five hundred, of crew and soldiers; with passengers say six hundred as a fair average. The proportion of sick and dead is not moderate, although they thought it "not much".

[3] *Page* 28. The "ours" refers to the Jesuits on board.

[4] *Page* 28. Hidden; secret.

[5] *Page* 28. Here "boiled", "cooked by boiling"; constantly used so in the Bible, for instance.

[1] *Page* 29. Also Sacatora, Secutra, Socotera, Scotra, Sechutera, Sokotora (in the middle of the nineteenth century), and many others. They all stand for our present Socotra, and if it really is to be traced to the Sanskrit *Sukhadhara*, "Abode of Bliss", they are certainly, most of them, nearer the mark.

[2] *Page* 29. That is, to run as northerly as possible.

[3] *Page* 29. Of running ashore anywhere on the coasts of Arabia or Persia.

[4] *Page* 29. The steersman or captain; a sense now obsolete.

[1] *Page* 30. The coin was the Portuguese *vintem*, still extant and worth then somewhere about twopence. Linschoten men-

tions this creature and links it with the coin, under the spelling "vintin", in the old English edition of his Travels. No closer identification seems probable; "a certain sea-beast" says the standard Dutch edition of Linschoten, "fish of Portugal" the leading Portuguese encyclopedia, and there is nothing more definite anywhere that I have been able to find. The *vintem* was marked with the wheel of Saint Catherine; this, its size of a penny, say, downwards, and the fact that it floated on the surface of the sea near India, are clues which may lead to future identification.

[2] *Page* 30. In Portugal.

[3] *Page* 30. Here both Moor and Cafre are used in the general sense of negro or negroid, though perhaps with a vague and uncertain distinction between the Mohammadan Moor and the non-Mohammadan Cafre (Cafre is from the Arabic *kafir*, infidel, impious wretch). The negro sense of "Moor" is seen in the later "Blackamoor"; we shall find it clearly used in a quite other sense later in the Text.

[4] *Page* 30. Any narrow strip of fabric, a usual meaning of the word then; we have it still in "boot-lace"

[5] *Page* 30. Palm-wine is the liquor, says Peter Mundy half a century later, "we called Toddy, or rather Tari". It was something like "new white wine, both in colour and taste; pleasant and wholesome", and had its name *tari* from the *tar* tree or Palmyra-palm, *Borassus flabellifer*, a chief source of it.

[6] *Page* 30. Our coco-nut, *cocos nucifera*. The word is the Spanish and Portuguese *coco*, a "bogey", from the three black marks at the end which can be viewed as a grotesque face; our "cocoa-nut" is a modern laziness of thinking.

[1] *Page* 31. Letters of this sort, almost in common form, sometimes in blank, were hopefully issued by Elizabeth to her voyagers or merchant-adventurers for possible delivery to potentates anywhere, legendary, vaguely-reputed or actual. It is not known that either of these particular letters was ever delivered.

[2] *Page* 31. Jalaluddin Akbar, the Great Mughal of this time, whose reign—1556–1605—synchronised nearly with that of Elizabeth. His full style was Muhammad Akbar, called Jalaluddin (Glory of the Faith). The spelling in the Text is constant in the 1598 Hakluyt; Ecebar and Ekber are others of the several variants found in old travellers and historians. The 1589 Hakluyt has "Yeladin el Kubar".

[3] *Page* 31. The modern Cambay. The State is now Gujarat, but the town of Cambay still stands—on the Gulf of Cambay. Other old spellings are Cambaietta, Cambeth, Cambaet—the last closer to its native original, Khambat.

[4] *Page* 31. Eagerness, desire. We retain this shade of sense, negatively, in "disaffection".

[1] *Page* 32. A form of "beholden" due to grammatical confusion; it was very common in the seventeenth century and did not die away until the eighteenth.

[2] *Page* 32. Thank, reward, or show gratitude to. No longer used in this sense, but we retain the idea in "gratuity".

[1] *Page* 33. I have placed the first "but that" in parentheses. One is clearly redundant, but both appear as they stand in the 1589 and 1598 Hakluyt.

[1] *Page* 34. Urgently, earnestly.

[2] *Page* 34. Tripolis is the Italian form of the Arabic Tarabulus; the "s" is now commonly dropped. The path our travellers followed from here to Basra is the great trade channel to the East long in the jealous occupation of the Venetians, who have left their traces to this day in the current Italianised forms of many place-names; we shall meet more of them as we go.

[3] *Page* 34. Babylon throughout our text is the modern Baghdad, and this was the customary nomenclature of ages. Sometimes Baghdad is distinguished as "New Babylon" and the real Babylon as "Old Babylon". A certain unmeant humour is folded into Purchas's marginal note :—"Babilon

(so vulgarly but falsely it is called) the true name is Bagdet." As "Bagdet" it very often appears on old maps.

[4] *Page* 34. Usually now Basra, though there are many variants. The Arabic name was El Basrah, and the l of the article may have influenced the early Italian form "Balsora", which gives Eldred his. The Portuguese turned the Italian form into "Baçora", and this again gave us our own late spelling Bussorah—still, in one shape or another, not quite defunct.

[5] *Page* 34. February 12th. The *Tiger* lay in the Pool somewhere not far below London Bridge and dropped down the river to Gravesend, sailing from there the next day. See Newbery's letter.

[6] *Page* 34. They arrived in the road the day before (see pages 38 and 40) but apparently lay aboard all night and landed on May Day early in the morning—Maying began at dawn or sooner, if you held by the rules.

[1] *Page* 35. We might say "the hostel of the English". "Fondeghi" is the early Italian *fondaco*, which had long held the special meaning of a mercantile establishment and lodging-house in a foreign country; "factory", in its old sense of a trader's or factor's headquarters, illustrates the idea of the thing. Such establishments, each devoted to a separate nation, were common in commercial centres frequented by bodies of foreign merchants; an elaborate example is our own Steelyard in old London, which flourished down to the reign of Edward VI as the privileged fortress, residence, club and warehouse at once of the German merchants of the Hanseatic League. The word comes from the Arabic *fanduk*, "a public hostel for traders and their wares"; it still means an "inn" in Sicily. "Fondeghi" suggests the Italian plural, but I suspect here a direct version of *fanduk* with the usual Syrian thickening of the K to G; *kelek*, for instance, is commonly pronounced "keleg".

[2] *Page* 35. Here, "separate"; a much older meaning

(and more correct) than our general present one of an undefined smallish number. The old sense is still retained in law-language. As used again at the end of the paragraph it has either its present meaning or that of "various", "different"

[3] *Page* 35. Lebanon.

[4] *Page* 35. There are really seven—Burj-el-Mechti, el-Arbain, en-Nahr, es-Seba, et-Takkiyeh, es-Seraya and el-Maghr. Two were apparently built later than this date; at any rate, only five are shown on a French engraving of 1615.

[5] *Page* 35. A corruption of the Turkish *yeni cheri*, "new troops". The Janissaries were a body of regular troops, formed in 1330 and composed of Christian prisoners, and the children of Christian parents, forcibly converted to or trained in Mohammadanism; and so recruited, they remained the pest and the only standing army of Turkey until their disbandment by slaughter in 1826. Probably the forts were held by an *orta*, the division answering roughly to our company and, at a low peace strength, sometimes numbering about a hundred, though mostly more.

[6] *Page* 35. These are the existing dunes of Er-Raml, to the south of the Greek and English Cemeteries. They have relented in their advance and the prophecy is still a prophecy.

[7] *Page* 35. This, the common old spelling of Bristol, is also the more correct, for the name is the Anglo-Saxon *Bricg-stow*, "the place of the Bridge".

[1] *Page* 36. Haven, roadstead. From the Anglo-Saxon *rad*, "a riding", a "road" is a place where one rides, whether in a ship or on a horse.

[2] *Page* 36. The present Hamah, on the Orontes river.

[3] *Page* 36. Here, growing cotton. We meet it later with another meaning not so simple.

[4] *Page* 36. The trade in oak-galls for dyers is still a valuable one in Syria.

[5] *Page* 36. The citadel hill of Hamah has now been stripped

bare of all cut stones for building work in the town below, so it is not likely that the inscription will ever be seen again. The "many men" may have been lost when the Turkish sultan Selim I took Syria from the Mamluk Sultan of Egypt in 1516.

[1] *Page* 37. That is, "inland", "without water-borne traffic"

[2] *Page* 37. It still stands in its splendour; its great gate alone makes it perhaps the most triumphantly beautiful castle in the world.

[3] *Page* 37. Rich orchards still lie along Aleppo's small river Kuweik.

[4] *Page* 37. Richard Hakluyt was born in 1553 at Eyton or Yatton, in Herefordshire, and was at Westminster School from 1564 to 1570. While there, the sight of a map at the chambers of a cousin in the Middle Temple—which was out of bounds—and the instruction from the cousin which followed lighted the passion which consumed him for the rest of his life. He began to preach navigation and geography when he went up to Christ Church, Oxford; learnt French, Spanish, Portuguese and Italian—in addition to the standard Greek and Latin—in order to read accounts of voyages; delivered lectures on navigational matters to merchants and seamen, and read all available French seafaring literature while Chaplain to the English Embassy in Paris from 1583 to 1588. His ambition was to copy the log and cross-examine the Master of every ship that sailed, and he did accumulate an amazing wealth of documents himself and bequeath the tradition of preserving such things, whereas the records of voyages before his time were nearly all lost or forgotten. He was Archdeacon of Westminster when he died in 1616, but his real religion is expressed in the great "Principal Navigations of the English Nation", the first version of which appeared in one volume in 1589, and the completed version, enlarged to three volumes, in 1598, 1599 and 1600. It is agreeable to know that his

family was an old one at Yatton of the purest English stock; the provider of many sheriffs and Members of Parliament and so leaving ample records. The Dutch flavour of the name is a spelling accident; the original form and pronunciation was Hacklewit or Hacklett. He was probably the founder of the British Empire.

[1] *Page* 38. Eldred says the 21st; Newbery twice says the 20th; both were careful men, but perhaps Newbery was the more fussily careful, so he may be right. Fitch, characteristically, gives no date at all.

[2] *Page* 38. Abulfeda, of the family of Saladin, in 1310 became governor of that Hamah the travellers have just passed through and afterwards successively its prince and sultan, ruling excellently and encouraging all learning until his death in 1331. His work on Geography—the "Cosmography" of Hakluyt's desire—was famous and still valued long after Newbery wrote, though no part of it seems to have appeared in any Western tongue for another seventy years. At Hamah in the small ruined Mosque of *El Hayyat*, "The Mosque of Snakes", is still his marble tomb, carved with the record of his death.

[3] *Page* 38. That given at the beginning of our text.

[4] *Page* 38. This may be Francisco Fernand or Fernandez, the Jesuit; who was sent out to India in 1573, was appointed to certain ecclesiastical offices in Goa in 1575, and was ultimately murdered in Chittagong at the beginning of the seventeenth century. He has left two Catechisms written in Bengali. The "note" may have been such another letter as those of Thomas Stevens and Frey Peter.

[5] *Page* 38. The Turkish form of our "pasha", which comes, apparently by way of the other old spelling "bashaw" (itself, perhaps, mixed up with the Turkish "*bash*", a "head", "chief"), from the Persian *padshah*, "king", or better, "emperor". A bassa is a governor of a province or some other loosely defined high dignitary.

NOTES

[6] *Page* 38. This might be one of several places. Ramadi on the Euphrates is not impossible, and Er Remtheh in Syria, which stands at the intersection of many ways on the Darb el Hajj—the great Pilgrims' Road from Damascus to Mecca—is likely enough, but certainty is difficult. All the Palestine Ramehs seem improbable.

[7] *Page* 38. This pleasant Italianate form of Damascus is common in English literature at least as late as "Paradise Lost", but our usual spelling is certainly nearer the original Arabic Dimeshk esh Sham.

[1] *Page* 39. Erzeroum, by early topographers spelled Arziron, Alzarome, Carztron and many other ways, and Trebizond, sometimes also Trabisonda. They are something over a hundred miles apart.

[2] *Page* 39. The Peace of Amasia had been concluded between Turkey and Persia in 1555 but war began again certainly in 1576 and broils on the frontier probably went on most of the time, so "eight years" would be fairly accurate.

[3] *Page* 39. Keeping, guardianship; "tuition" bore this meaning then and had nothing to do with teaching. In Scots law—as in the Latin original and in the Authorised Version of the Bible—a "tutor" is still the "guardian" of a legal infant.

[1] *Page* 40. Of Gibraltar.

[2] *Page* 40. Barret was at this time English Consul at Aleppo; we shall hear the end of him from Eldred.

[3] *Page* 40. Some sort of bale or package. "Ball" and "bale" go back to the same root and were not rigidly distinguished at this time.

[4] *Page* 40. Manner; a constant older meaning. We are apt now to think of the word as indicating that which is ranked or in sequence, but we retain a lingering of the earlier sense in the phrase "in good order" though even here disguised by association with the image of a body of soldiers.

NOTES

[1] *Page* 41. That is, the despatch of *The Tiger* back to England laden and the onward journey of Newbery and his companions.

[2] *Page* 41. Coral.

[3] *Page* 41. For beads or other ornaments; there was a good deal of poor quality glass made at Aleppo.

[4] *Page* 41. The value of the ducat varied considerably, but may be taken as round about four shillings at this time.

[5] *Page* 41. Profits are now "estimated", but a house is "rated" still.

[1] *Page* 42. The Text word is from the Spanish *cargazon*, not, probably, the more familiar French *cargaison*. Our present "cargo"—also from the Spanish—did not come into use till about eighty years later.

[2] *Page* 42. He would be thinking chiefly of the Barbary Corsairs, who from their principal strongholds of Tunis, Algiers and Tripoli (the other Tripoli in Africa) scourged the Mediterranean until Blake thrashed them into a kind of quietness in 1655. Merchant-ships often did sail in company in order to be strong enough to fight them off.

[3] *Page* 42. Or madyne, maydin, medin and other spellings; a silver coin worth eleven maravedis, or three-halfpence, more or less, of our money.

[1] *Page* 43. Bir, Biredjik or Birejik on the Euphrates; it was Bira in the time of the Crusades. It is at the limit of navigation on that river, and is the crossing point of the great caravan route from Syria through Aleppo to Baghdad. Sixteen big ferry boats were kept there, and caravans of more than five thousand camels would cross by them. Tradition says that the Patriarch Abraham lost many cattle here in fording the Euphrates. It is now a place of about 15,000 people.

[2] *Page* 43. The Accadian name of the Euphrates was *Pura*, the "water", and the Babylonian Semites turned this into *Purat*. The early Persians gave this a twist so that it might

mean something in their own tongue and it became *Hufrat*, the "very broad" river, in later Persian, *Phrat*. The Arabs turned this into *Al Furat* or *Frat*, "the sweet water", its present Arabic name. With so much folk-etymology at work it is tempting to imagine a little more. *Al Furat* is so nearly right Arabic for "a thousand heads" that Europeans (Newbery at least of the party knew Arabic) or even some Arab tribes might conceivably take that to be its meaning. Above Birejik the Euphrates does gather up countless tributaries, so the name, in any case, is not merely figurative and might be exactly ascertained with further research.

[3] *Page* 43. These are the "danecs" mentioned later by Fitch.

[4] *Page* 43. A "shallow" and a "shoal" of fish were once two quite different words; our forefathers provided matter of confusion for us when they mixed them up and began to spell "shold" as "shoal", which is the corrupted "shallow" by way of such forms as "shalwe"; they would have done better, moreover, to keep to a "school" of fish—which is really the proper form of the word and has nothing whatever to do with "shoal" in its meaning of a "shallow".

[5] *Page* 43. An Italian form of Felluja or Kalat Felluja, on the Eastern bank of the Euphrates almost due West of Baghdad, which is thirty-five miles or so away as the crow flies. It was also spelt Feluge, Feloge, Feluchia and otherwise and has a fine confusion of modern spellings, with Felugia still sometimes among them.

[1] *Page* 44. "Are accustomed to" We have lost this neat and handy present tense, though we curiously retain the past tense "used to do" with a certain vagueness as to its meaning.

[2] *Page* 44. The "churned milk" is butter, and to churn milk by shaking it in a skin bag is one of the most widespread, as it is perhaps the very oldest, of all methods of churning.

[3] *Page* 44. Gipsies, which is merely "Egyptians" disguised. Though in fact of some indeterminate Indian origin they were long supposed to have come from Egypt. "Gipsy" instead of "Egyptian" was first used in 1600, by Shakespeare.

[1] *Page* 45. It is about fifty miles across.

[2] *Page* 45. That is, in the "short desert" generally, not on the line across it from Felluja to Baghdad; the site of Babylon is over a hundred miles down-stream. He may have omitted to mention this deliberately in order to speak with more relevance of a place the name of which was still a world's wonder.

[1] *Page* 46. The height of the tower of old St. Paul's was 260 feet; the lead-and-wood steeple itself—another 260 feet —was destroyed by lightning in June, 1561, and never rebuilt. Among the English this was long reputed to be the height of the ruined "Babel"; or "Babil", as the Arabs called it.

[2] *Page* 46. This was the method of building the walls of Babylon, according to Herodotus, who says that they used the bitumen of Hit for cement and laid the mats of canes at every thirtieth course; except that the mats are at smaller intervals it is the method found to exist in many Babylonian ruins. The bricks are sun-dried.

[3] *Page* 46. Called so commonly and inaccurately; Mosul is on the western bank of the Tigris, Nineveh was on the eastern, though not far away.

[1] *Page* 47. These are the *keleks* or *kellegs* of to-day and were old in the time of Herodotus, who, however, mixed them up with the coracles or *ghufas.* The skins are blown up by a reed through one of the legs and by the legs, chiefly, they are tied to a light framework of slender poles. A few trunks of walnut or poplar sawn in half are laid on the framework, and all may be finished at will with a decking of boards and a hut of mats on a reed frame. Practice varies, but generally a hundred skins will make a raft big enough for six people with

baggage. They are still dismantled and the rest of it exactly as Eldred says.

[2] *Page* 47. There were about thirty boats at this time, twelve feet beam and twelve feet apart, with a timbered causeway. The bridge was cast apart in mid-stream at night so that the current laid one half against each bank.

[3] *Page* 47. Several other letters will be found addressed to this mysterious "G. S.". In his marginal note regarding them Purchas says that they were found among the papers of William Hareborne (who was English Ambassador at Constantinople at this time) with annotations in his hand; that is point one in the inference that they were addressed to Hareborne. Point two is that at the end of this letter Eldred talks of "our county, Norfolk"; he and Hareborne were both Norfolk men. Point three is that the style of address is the same in the "G. S." letters as in those explicitly directed to Hareborne—one suited, that is, to a high dignitary. The fact that Hareborne was not a peer and that "Lordship" is used means nothing; it was a not unusual piece of expansive courtesy in such circumstances and had about the same significance as "Excellency". It is all so plain that there would never have been two thoughts about the matter but for that "G. S." label; this is probably one more of Purchas's abundant editorial sins.

[1] *Page* 48. Obsolete form of "Kerseys", and kerseys, as here mentioned, were not merely the coarse, ribbed woollen fabrics so named but fixed measures of such fabric, contrasted with cloth. By Statute a kersey was eighteen yards long and a yard and a nail in width, while a broadcloth was twenty-four yards long by two yards wide; about thirty years later than our text three kerseys were reckoned equal to one cloth.

[2] *Page* 48. He means dogs who had to be bribed—Turkish authorities, Arab blackmailers and so forth. More will be heard of them later.

NOTES

[1] *Page* 49. Literally, "as good market"; the French *bon marché* has the same idea. Our present "cheap", alone and meaning "not dear", seems to have been only once so used before this date, and did not begin to creep into general and continued use till some years later. The phrase needs careful watching: so excellent an editor as G. W. Forrest once stuck a comma between "better" and "cheap" in quoting some old passage and made unintelligible nonsense of the simple statement that certain goods were "cheaper".

[2] *Page* 49. This passage stands thus in the 1625 Purchas, but either "one hundred and twenty pieces of Carsies and a half" or "a half-some Tin" would make a more satisfactory reading; which of these emendations would represent the intended meaning it is impossible to say. The meaning of "some" will appear later.

[3] *Page* 49. A "scarlet" was in older English a broadcloth simply, irrespective of colour. The exact history of the word is doubtful, but it is certainly connected or mixed up with the Persian sakallat, "a woollen stuff". It has several forms and is found even as "sackcloth" at a later date than our text.

[4] *Page* 49. The rotello, rotola, rotilo, rotula, rottula, rottil, rottel and several other spellings, is a weight of about one pound avoirdupois. Its ultimate derivation is from the Arabic *ratl*, a pound. As the "ratlo" it lasted on in Goa till modern times, and still survives in Southern Italy and Sicily.

[5] *Page* 49. Our present "County", and in much more common use than this until long after the date of our text.

[1] *Page* 50. William Hareborne or Harborne was a bailiff of Yarmouth in 1572; Osborne and Staper's emissary to Turkey and their factor in Constantinople in 1577, where he procured the "first heroical letters" from the "Grand Signior" inviting Elizabeth's friendship. Various privileges and treaties he obtained from the Turks, with whom he always had great influence, helped to put England on a level with

Venice, France and other nations and led to the founding of the Turkey Company in 1579. Elizabeth appointed him her ambassador at Constantinople in November, 1582. He returned in 1588; settled at Mundham in Norfolk, and died there in September, 1617.

[2] *Page* 50. Wherever found in our earlier literature the "Grand Signior", "Grand Turk", "Great Turk" or the like is the Sultan of Turkey.

[3] *Page* 50. This is Samuel Purchas, the disciple (at a distance) and literary Executor of Richard Hakluyt, whose undigested material he published, with other matter, in 1625, under the title of "Hakluytus Posthumus, or Purchas his Pilgrims".

[4] *Page* 50. By a late computation there are in India one hundred and eighty *leading* tongues.

[1] *Page* 51. Abushahr; the modern port of Bushire, on the Persian Gulf.

[2] *Page* 51. That is, an interpreter.

[3] *Page* 51. Also Nostrane and others; the Arabic *Nazrani*, a term for "Christian" having the same intense flavour of contempt as its original, Nazarene. The "t" may have intruded through confusion with "Nestorian"; the Nestorians are Eastern Christians despised not only by Easterns but by other Christians.

[4] *Page* 51. Evilly inclined. The Anglo-Saxon *laewede* meant "belonging to the laity", hence "ignorant", as opposed to the learned man, the clerk; from that it came to mean many sorts of turpitude before reaching its current sense. We shall find it meaning something like "ill-conditioned" later in the text.

[5] *Page* 51. Or Bateman; a weight of about seven pounds five ounces avoirdupois.

[1] *Page* 52. This "which" appears in the original Hakluyt, but should certainly be either "I" or "we" preceded

by a full stop. The context makes it evident that George Gill did not arrive at Felugia and the *Tiger* could not.

[2] *Page* 52. Scarcely, or with difficulty, to be obtained; the sense is not directly that of a scantiness of camels.

[1] *Page* 53. Turbith, turpeth, turbit and other spellings: the Indian jalap—obtained from the root of a kind of convolvulus, *Ipomoea Turpethum*—a drug more esteemed then, perhaps, than now.

[2] *Page* 53. Indigo; from the Spanish *anil*, which is the Arabic *al nyl*, "blue", with the "l" of the article assimilated to the initial "n" in the usual Arabic manner.

[3] *Page* 53. Indigo was sold by the package called in India *churl*, a term specially used in this commerce. It is from the Spanish *churla*, "a bag of cinnamon". In English weight it was about a hundred and thirty pounds avoirdupois or rather more.

[1] *Page* 54. "Their Conducts" is here equivalent to "the goods convoyed by them", "their Convoys".

[2] *Page* 54. Long Pepper is the fruit-spike of the woody-stemmed climbing plants *Piper longum* and *Piper officinarum*. The fruits form a compact mass on the spike, which is gathered and sold whole; hence the name. They are used for pickling, culinary and medicinal purposes. The Black and White Pepper of commerce are the fruits, differently treated, of the spongey-stemmed climber *Piper Nigrum*; the fruits of this are not so closely packed on the spike, and dried and rubbed off become the familiar peppercorn.

[3] *Page* 54. Syndye—also spelt Cinde, Sindu, Scinde, Cindy and in other ways—is the port of Diul-Sindi on a mouth of the Indus near Laribandar or Karachi. The distance is about a hundred leagues too short but there is no doubt about the place, and that being so the "feathers" are clearly *chowries*, or yak-tails, which were sometimes called feathers and were a great trade at this port.

NOTES

[1] *Page* 55. The Crusades made the Levant acquainted with the Franks or French first and chiefly of Europeans, and thereabouts and in India the word is still used for a European generally, in some form like the Indian *feringhi*, Persian *farangi*, Arabic *faranji*, *frangue*, *fringi* and others.

[2] *Page* 55. Keeping the exact Italian form, since the word —like most of our banking and financial terms—came to us from the Italians.

[3] *Page* 55. The second "that" would be better away, but both are given in the 1625 Purchas.

[4] *Page* 55. "Magosine" is Magazine, then a place for the storage of merchandise; and "cave" is a storage-cellar. "Cravancera" is caravanserai, or "inn".

[5] *Page* 55. If; the strengthened form "and if" or "an if" was quite usual.

[1] *Page* 56. A form of "lose" that did not become obsolete among the learned until near the eighteenth century.

[2] *Page* 56. Forbid. A forbidden thing is still *chose défendue* in French.

[3] *Page* 56. Philip of Spain had managed to snatch the throne of Portugal in 1580, but the East Indies were a long way away, and the Portuguese, though they had to put up with Philip, did not want his interloping subjects there and managed to make the long voyage too long for most of them. Philip had too much trouble on his hands and too little money in them to force matters very much at first, and the Armada catastrophe left him in no case at all to do anything.

[1] *Page* 57. Ozeah is El Ozeir, where there is a reputed tomb of the Prophet Ezra; Zecchiah may be the "Zakieh" shown on D'Anville's map of 1751, about ten miles above Kurna.

[2] *Page* 57. Curna is our Kurna, where the Tigris and Euphrates unite to make the Shatt el Arab. The tides are

actually felt about thirty miles beyond Kurna, and the country towards and around Basra is almost a vast date-grove.

[1] *Page* 58. Indigo. The form "indico" was that in general use until about 1650.

[2] *Page* 58. Calecut cloth is our calico, and the name comes from the Indian port of Calicut on the Malabar coast. Early spellings are very various and include such forms as kalyko, calocowe and callaga.

[3] *Page* 58. The *bagalas* of the Persian Gulf still have their planks sewn like this, and in some ways it makes a very good job—the ships are supple, for instance, and strain less in riding through a sea.

[4] *Page* 58. Oakum for caulking. The text spelling is etymologically more exact and less misleading, for the word means fibrous matter teased or "combed out"—the Scots dialect retains "Kame"—and has nothing to do with "oak"

[5] *Page* 58. Shreds or shavings. The great authority of the Oxford English Dictionary must here be questioned (and in respect of this very passage of the text) though with much deference. You could not caulk a ship with "fragments" or "splinters"—unless you give an unsuitable sense to "fragment". Shakespeare has "shive", "a thin slice", and there is "shiver" with the same meaning, both from the Icelandic *skifa*, "a slice". The entry would appear to have been made in forgetfulness of the fact that the "shiverings" were used for caulking and rope spinning.

[6] *Page* 58. Our Bahrein. The pearl-fisheries are still perhaps the finest in the world and in annual export-value reach something like half-a-million pounds sterling or more. The "six days' sailing" is roughly four hundred miles.

[1] *Page* 59. We should expect "a religious" here, but it is "religious" in the 1589 and 1598 Hakluyt; both those editions have "John" Story though Fitch calls him "James"

With his greater intimacy Fitch was the more likely to be right, so the "John" is probably a slip of Eldred's.

[2] *Page* 59. Fitch says the 5th, also that they were put in prison on the 9th. It is impossible to say who was right, but Newbery gives the impression of a precise man whilst there is a casual and easy flavour about Fitch which may have extended to his dates; at any rate he seldom inserts any during his Indian wanderings, though it is true he may have lost count.

[1] *Page* 60. The Captain of Ormus was the Portuguese governor. The post was held at this time by Mathias de Albuquerque.

[2] *Page* 60. In 1580 Philip of Spain had intrigued and bullied his way to the throne of Portugal, on the failure of the royal line, in face of many claimants with much better titles. One of these was Don Antonio, grandson of Emmanuel the Great. He lost two battles against Philip, fled into exile in England in 1581, and was used by Elizabeth as a tool in her Spanish manipulations until 1589. Philip held his new throne chiefly by main force and none too strongly, and his jealous fear of English intruders upon the East Indian preserves may reasonably have been increased by the suspicion—promptly, one can be sure, transmitted to Goa—that they were working for Don Antonio.

[3] *Page* 60. Sir Edward Osborne and Richard Staper, who had planned and mainly paid for the voyage.

[1] *Page* 61. The lack of formal beginning and the abrupt manner of this letter are worth noting as a mark of furtive haste in the writing and, perhaps, some stress of nerves.

[2] *Page* 61. This "Andrew" was perhaps the "Italian which came from Aleppo"; see Newbery's letter to Poore from Goa, 20th January, 1584.

[3] *Page* 61. In the 1598 edition of Hakluyt, and naturally in the MacLehose edition, which is based on it, this reads "possible", but in the 1589 Hakluyt it is "possibly"; so,

with this authority, as "possibly" is clearly right I have restored it.

[1] *Page* 62. Plans. "Plat" still seems to be used in America in the sense of map, plan or chart.

[2] *Page* 62. Viceroy—the Portuguese form of the word.

[3] *Page* 62. "Messe" is the Italian *messo*, "a messenger"; so the phrase is "express messenger".

[1] *Page* 63. Condition. The word had nothing to do with property originally.

[2] *Page* 63. The passage stands thus in the 1625 Purchas, but there is evidently something wrong with it. "Is" instead of "as" makes it fairly right, but would be better between "place" and "only": "being this place is only as a thoroughfare" looks as if it were what he wrote or intended to write.

[3] *Page* 63. "Make a market".

[4] *Page* 63. He, we, you, they mindeth or departeth would be the correct form of conjugation in much older English than our text; it is curious to find so late a survival of it. Unless indeed, "they" should have been "he", as the following "his" indicates. Purchas was a careless editor.

[1] *Page* 64. A judge or magistrate; the Arabic *kadi*.

[1] *Page* 65. A "some" is the Italian *soma*, which means in general any kind of load or burden and often a mule-load or—as here—camel-load. From the camel-load it was taken to mean also a more or less definite though very variable weight, roughly equivalent to five hundred pounds avoirdupois. Our text seems to intend now the one meaning, now the other; which, can be judged by the context where the word occurs.

[2] *Page* 65. Fusses of cloves were clove-stalks, from the Italian *fusti*. They had some weakish clove flavour about them and were an important enough substitute article of commerce in days when the clove itself was so eagerly sought and not too easily come by. Their value was about a third that of the clove proper.

NOTES

[3] *Page* 65. A "b" at the end of "turban" is quite right; the word is the Persian *dulband*, Turkish *tulbend*, from which last, by way of another old spelling, "tulipant", comes our "tulip"—really, therefore, the "turban-flower". We do still talk of the "turban ranunculus".

[4] *Page* 65. Porcelain. Puselen, purcellain and purselane are other variant spellings.

[5] *Page* 65. The "others" refers to "news", which began life with the plural meaning retained by it until fairly late in the nineteenth century.

[1] *Page* 66. The French *moutons*. We retain the old usage in "mutton-headed", which, naturally, means "sheep-headed" and has no reference to butcher's meat.

[1] *Page* 67. The popular pronunciation of Magdalene was that exemplified in Magdalen at Oxford and Magdalene at Cambridge, and in our present word "maudlin", its derivative. Eldred certainly had this pronunciation in mind, for Maudlin is a name confusedly given to several herbs—Costmary, Alecost, Cost or Tansy, *Tanacetum Balsamita*; Agrimony, *Agrimonia Eupatoria*, and Milfoil or Yarrow, *Achillea Ageratum*, which last is specifically Sweet Maudlin and is most probably the plant the camels fed on or a close relation of it. Wormwood is *Artemisia Absinthium*.

[2] *Page* 67. The modern Hit, famous for its bitumen-springs from the remotest antiquity. Heredotus mentions it under the name of Is. The bitumen was that once used for cementing the Assyrian and Babylonian buildings, as it is still used for caulking and pitching the Mesopotamian *ghufas* and *danecs*. The springs lie close under the Hoda Sanjak hills, on the river side of them.

[3] *Page* 67. Near enough to the Arabic *Bab el Jahannam*, the most exact of modern transliterations, and in its latter part even closer to the Hebrew original *Ge Hinnom*, the "Valley of Hinnom" near Jerusalem, which was at first a place of

sacrifice to Moloch and afterwards the city's refuse destructor, whence at length our present *Gehenna*, "hell"

[1] *Page* 68. The Italian form of Abu Risha, which seems to have been the family name of a line of Amirs of Ana, on the Euphrates. The particular Amir whom Fitch heard about would be Ahmad Abu Risha. They and their Analis were all thieves and notorious blackmailers—in the older and more respectable sense of the word.

[2] *Page* 68. The Dead Sea.

[1] *Page* 69. It is not easy to understand why we prefer our less correct "Bengal". Other early European spellings are Banzelo, Bemgala and Banghella ; all represent the Sanskrit *Vangalam*, from another form of which, Vanga, the Mohammadan geographers took their "Bang"

[2] *Page* 69. Such a place may or may not have existed, but he never says that he went there. He does say later that the king of Serrepore was called Chondery. It looks like the mistake of some careless assistant who put in headings for Hakluyt.

[3] *Page* 69. Imahay is the Jamahey, afterwards more fully mentioned. Zeilan is Ceylon ; other old spellings are Sailan, Selonc, Seilan—all closer than ours to the original *Silan*, the native colloquial form of the Sanskrit *Sinhala*, "Abode of Lions".

[1] *Page* 70. Financed, fitted out, equipped.

[1] *Page* 71. Turkestan, not Turkey.

[1] *Page* 72. This is probably the tower of Akr Kuf, often mistaken by early travellers for the real Babel, which is a hundred miles south. The description would do fairly well for either. Akr Kuf lies about ten miles from Baghdad, rather north of the direct track to Felluja.

[2] *Page* 72. This is Hit again.

[1] *Page* 73. Some other spellings are cairo, cair, cayar, and kiar. It is our "coir", the fibre of the coco-nut, from which

rope is commonly made. In its original Malayalam form, *kayar*, the word does mean "cord", and not merely a stuff from which cord is made.

[2] *Page* 73. Shining, lustrous. A poetic adjective now, in this sense; a practical everyday one then.

[1] *Page* 74. Our present spelling, Hormuz, is a more correct transliteration of the Arabic than is the Portuguese form, Ormuz. The description is sufficiently exact. The existing city stands on the island of Jerun, about twelve miles from the site of the old mainland city and four from the nearest shore; there is no fresh water other than the rain-water stored in tanks, and there are mountains of salt—almost.

[2] *Page* 74. Persian carpets, not what we now understand by tapestry. In old French, *tapisserie*—from which our word comes—was strictly "carpeting", and at the date of our text carpets were still chiefly used for covering tables and so forth, scarcely at all as floor-covering. Thus we get our present colloquial "on the carpet", which fundamentally involves the meaning of laying the written statement of a case on the table for judgment; it is a near cousin of "putting your cards on the table".

[3] *Page* 74. The trade in horses between Hormuz and India is a great one to this day. The bales of cheaper squashed dates for the Indian bazars sometimes travel in the same vessels below the horses without effect on their vendibility—from an Indian point of view.

[4] *Page* 74. "Jewels", "ornaments"; our present "locket" is a diminutive of it and meant originally a patterned arrangement of small jewels.

[5] *Page* 74. The custom of perforating the ear-lobes and enlarging the aperture to a greater or less extent is widely spread in the East; we shall hear of it again several times.

[1] *Page* 75. The present Sind; so they made a coasting voyage of it.

NOTES

[2] *Page* 75. Bahadur Shah of Gujerat let the Portuguese build a fort at Diu in 1535; in 1545 the town and whole island became theirs and still remains so. The island is about seven miles by two.

[3] *Page* 75. The Straits of Bab-el-Mandeb; shown as the "Gates of Mecca" on Berthelot's map of 1635 and perhaps elsewhere.

[4] *Page* 75. The modern city of Cambay; see later note.

[5] *Page* 75. Here and throughout the remainder of the text "Gentiles" means any non-Mohammadan peoples of the East, in distinction to "Moors", who were the Mohammadans. "Gentile" is the Portuguese *gentio*, and "Moor" the Portuguese *moro*.

[6] *Page* 75. Not to be eaten, but for slaves. The practice was alleged of many parts of the East.

[7] *Page* 75. This is Bahadur Shah of Gujerat. He was not killed at the siege of Diu but murdered and thrown into the water while on a diplomatic visit to the Portuguese aboard their ships. They denied complicity in the deed, but historians are still unconvinced.

[1] *Page* 76. This represents the correct Hindi "Dilli"; "Dehli" is the Indo-Persian form; our modern "Delhi" is entirely wrong. The "h" through carelessness has slipped into the wrong place and through slackness has remained there.

[2] *Page* 76. Or tusks. Since they really are teeth it was not unnatural for all the early travellers to call them so.

[3] *Page* 76. Daman was sacked by the Portuguese in 1531 and taken by them finally in 1558; the town and its hundred and seventy square miles of territory still belong to them. Note that the word but one before "Daman" is "come" in the original Hakluyt also, and not "came" as might be expected. A misprint possibly.

[4] *Page* 76. Basaim is also spelt Bazim; it is the modern Bassein. The town and land round were ceded to the Por-

tuguese by Bahadur Shah in 1534; the Marathas took it from them in 1739. Tana is the modern Thana (which is correct), towards the northern end of Salsette Island, on the landward side. It became Portuguese in 1533 and was lost by them when Bassein was lost.

[5] *Page* 76. The mainland, as opposed to an island. The phrase will occur again.

[6] *Page* 76. The Nizam Shahi dynasty of Ahmadnagar was founded by that Nizam-ul-Mulk who was always called by the early travellers Xa-Maluco, Zemelluco or some such name. They used the same name, too, without distinction, for every ruler of the line, as in the similar cases of the Adil Shahi and Kutb Shahi dynasties and others. It is much as if we should say that the sovereign of England in 1530 was King Tudor or in 1670 King Stuart. The reigning prince at this time was Murtaza Nizam Shah I, 1565–1587, in whose domain Chaul stood; and the town "a little above" Chaul was Alibagh. The Portuguese had a factory at Chaul.

[7] *Page* 76. Sandal-wood; more will be heard of it later. The plural form is due not only to the fact that there were different kinds, but that sandal was often spoken of as "sanders", so the "s" came easily.

[8] *Page* 76. Jaggery; the coarse chocolate-coloured sugar made in India from the sappy juice—not the nut—of various kinds of palm-tree. The word is the Malayalam *chakkara*, Hindustani *jagri*, through the Portuguese form *jagara*.

[9] *Page* 76. Palm-tree; a commonly-used alternative, also spelled "pawmer". Both forms are from the French *palmier*, *paumier*; though this derivation is probably a good deal mixed up with "Palmyra". The famous abundant virtues of the Palm are accurately catalogued.

[1] *Page* 77. Distil. We now use "still" in this sense only as a noun—"illicit still", for instance.

[2] *Page* 77. The manner of collecting palm-wine is well

described. The "branch" which is cut and bound is the spathe or flowering shoot; this has its tip sliced off slantwise and its base ligatured and is then bruised by beating with a stick. The flow of juice begins in a few days and continues for about a fortnight at the rate of perhaps three quarts a day. It is "toddy" for not longer than four days or so; after that it turns sour, ferments, and is distilled into "arrack" just as Fitch says, though what his "dried raisins" are I do not know.

[3] *Page* 77. Nandi, the sacred bull of Siva, who has been for long one of the most popular gods of the crowded Hindu pantheon, and the symbolic animal is often worshipped indifferently with the god. The cow shares the bull's sacredness and has an original and special sacredness of her own, and the Hindu's horror of killing or eating her is sufficiently known. The cow's holiness extends to her excrements, and to smear walls and floor of a house with *gobar*, a paste of cow-dung, is not only to cleanse and purify it physically in the most perfect way but to render it ceremonially pure and, as it were, sanctified; such a double effect as might be obtained by scrubbing the Vatican, for instance, with holy water.

[4] *Page* 77. Vegetables generally

[5] *Page* 77. The famous custom of sati or suttee. The brief account is perfectly exact as far as it goes.

[1] *Page* 78. These animal hospitals are called Pinjrapol. Mostly supported by Jains, they were common in Gujerat and elsewhere in Western India in the seventeenth century. They began somewhere in the time of Asoka—say 250 B.C. It is quite true that a Hindu is proscribed by his religion from killing even a louse, as Fitch has just said; it may not be equally true that, as many European travellers have averred, beggars were hired for the purpose of affording sustenance to the lice and other vermin which happened to be patients at these hospitals, though it is quite certain that such creatures were inmates in some sort of capacity and were tended somehow.

NOTES

[2] *Page* 78. Food generally, not necessarily flesh-food. To "sit at meat" meant simply to sit down to a meal. The phrase "rabbits' meat" is sometimes heard still in country places.

[3] *Page* 78. Goa town and island were captured by Alfonso de Albuquerque in 1510 from the King of Bijapur, by whom Bardez and Salsette were ceded to the Portuguese in 1543; the three districts constituted the *Velhas Conquistas*—the Old Conquests; the remaining districts of the territory, which extends to about a thousand square miles in all, are known as the New Conquests. Goa is still Portuguese and the present city is at Panjim in the north-west part of Goa Island, while Old Goa was in the north-east. In its full splendour Old Goa (the city Fitch knew) was called *Goa Dourada*—Golden Goa; it is now ruined and desolate.

[4] *Page* 78. Cochin on the Malabar Coast; not to be confused (it has happened) with Cochin-China.

[5] *Page* 78. Thirty leagues too little; at a short reckoning it is four hundred miles.

[6] *Page* 78. The Adil Shahi dynasty of Bijapur was founded in 1489 by Yusuf Adil Khan, who changed his style "Khan" to "Shah"; in spite of the change he and the successive Kings of his line were referred to as "Adil Khan"—in various spellings—by European travellers long after Fitch. Alfonso de Albuquerque took Goa from Yusuf Adil Shah in 1510; Ibrahim Adil Shah II was the reigning King of the dynasty during Fitch's stay in India. His "chief city", Bisapor, is the present Bijapur.

[1] *Page* 79. A far older word than "German" among the English. The "Nazaranies" further on in the list are the "Nastraynes" once more.

[1] *Page* 80. The Portuguese silver coin *pardao*. A "*pardao xerafine*" was worth about four shillings, a "*pardao de larins*" about five; it is doubtful to which Newbery refers.

NOTES

[2] *Page* 80. The Rua Direita in Old Goa. It was the street of the great Cathedral, which still stands though the street is in ruins.

[3] *Page* 80. Maluco is the Moluccas, and Drake is Francis Drake ; he had been busy there about four years before.

[4] *Page* 80. Advocate-General. We have the Scots " Lord-Advocate ".

[1] *Page* 82. This is Jan Huyghen van Linschoten, who was born at Haarlem in 1563, began his travels at the age of sixteen ; spent some years in Spain, and went with the Portuguese East India fleet to Goa in September, 1583. He returned in 1589 and settled at Enkhuizen, where he died 8th February, 1611. His great book of voyages—translated into English in 1598—was for generations the standard authority on the navigation of the Cape route to the East Indies.

[2] *Page* 82. This is the Dutch Jesuit mentioned later by Linschoten.

[3] *Page* 82. December 21st.

[1] *Page* 83. The Portuguese *escrivão*, a " purser " or " supercargo " ; sometimes used as if it meant " recorder " or " registrar " simply.

[2] *Page* 83. As we should say, a " memorandum ".

[3] *Page* 83. That is, the bearer of this letter.

[1] *Page* 84. It will have been observed that the euphonic " an " is used before certain words such as " hundred ", " half ", " house ", which are now aspirated. In portions of the text extracted from Purchas some of these words appear with " a ", so usage may have changed by 1625. In the absence of such explicit authority as that, for instance, of Ben Jonson for " an host ", " an humble person ", it is, however, unsafe to draw conclusions about the English aspirate, since we may always have been as dull-eared and muddle-minded in this matter as we appear to be now, when we are capable of employing such illegal cacophonies as " a historian ", " a hotel ", " a

hussar", or such related absurdities as "an European", "an unique".

[2] *Page* 84. A guarantor or surety.

[3] *Page* 84. The chekin is what we now mostly call the sequin and sometimes zecchin, the Italian *zecchino*; a fair value for it would be about ten shillings. The word is from the Venetian *zeccha*, "a mint", which again is from the Arabic *sikka*, "a coining die". The larine or larin, from the Persian *lari*, was worth about a shilling. It was a coin very curiously made of a small rod of silver hammered slightly flat and then bent into a hairpin shape and sometimes so left; but sometimes the two ends were bent back again so that the whole thing became a kind of double fish-hook. Some kind of coin device was stamped on the two ends. The name is from Lar in Persia, the chief city of Laristan, where it was said to have been first coined. The *pardao* here was clearly the "pardao de larins" worth five shillings. Bearing these values in mind, and taking the crown at its present rate, there is entertainment in working out the profits made by the Captain of Ormus (and, incidentally, some of those Newbery expected to make), as detailed in the whole of this indignant passage.

[4] *Page* 84. This was the Italian *picco*; as the *pik* it is still a common cloth-measure in the Levant. It is variable to some extent, but may be taken as about twenty-eight inches.

[5] *Page* 84. The inflamed nature of some of the references to Michael Stropene is accounted for by the fact that, at Newbery's previous visit to Ormus in 1581, his Greek servant Jacomo had left his service for that of Stropene on the 7th of July, enticed, as Newbery suspected, by Stropene in order that he might be pumped of his English master's trade secrets. The suspicion was probably justified; it was a typical Venetian trick.

[1] *Page* 86. Crowded, especially when overcrowded. A good modern equivalent would be the dialect "cluttered".

NOTES

[1] *Page* 87. Petition, plead. The word was not confined to its present strictly legal sense till much later.

[1] *Page* 88. Despoiled, pilfered. We retain this sense in "the spoils of war".

[1] *Page* 89. The torture of having the hands tied behind the back and fastened to a rope, and being then hoisted up by that rope, let down suddenly, and stopped halfway with a jerk. It is the Italian *strappata*, "dragged" or "snatched" This is how they were to be "better sifted".

[2] *Page* 89. The River Mandavi, which separates Goa Island from Bardez.

[1] *Page* 90. Or caffylen and other spellings. The Arabic *kafila*, a "caravan".

[2] *Page* 90. In his "Voyages".

[3] *Page* 90. John Newbery; between September, 1580, and August, 1582.

[4] *Page* 90. "Advertisement" then meant—among other things—"admonition", "warning", "instruction"

[1] *Page* 91. Spied upon.

[2] *Page* 91. Cheated or swindled out of—a sense no longer used.

[3] *Page* 91. Fitch was right—see page 74—and Linschoten is wrong. The Portuguese records show that Mathias de Albuquerque took over the office of Captain from Gonçalo de Menezes in January, 1583.

[1] *Page* 92. Always, consistently. We have almost lost this shade of meaning.

[1] *Page* 95. "Sold", "disposed of". Goods were "uttered" then, coin (generally false) is "uttered" now. If we spelt it "outered" we should see the root-idea of all senses of the verb, which is from the Anglo-Saxon *utian*, "to put out", while utter, "extreme", is from the connected *utor*, "outer"

[2] *Page* 95. "To respect" is now to be in a state of mind;

earlier it indicated an outward physical action—as Linschoten has it, "showing great courtesy unto". For this sense we now have to employ some such circumlocution as 'pay respect to".

[1] *Page* 96. Our "disport", and commonly used in place of it down to the eighteenth century.

[2] *Page* 96. Bardez is one of the three districts comprised in the *Velhas Conquistas*, or Old Conquests, of the settlement of Goa; it lies northward of Goa Bay, across the Mandavi river.

[1] *Page* 97 The Hindi *Pathmar*, a 'courier", "running postman"

[2] *Page* 97. In the Mughal Empire, in Bijapur and in all the other Mohammadan realms, which in that day included approximately all India north of the Tungabhadra and Kistna Rivers.

[1] *Page* 98. The veneseander, or venetiander, was a gold coin worth here either eight or ten shillings, according to the kind of "pardawe" he means; the "pardawe Xerafine" would make it worth about eight, the "pardawe de larins", about ten.

[1] *Page* 99. A half-caste; from the Portuguese *mestiço*—or, as it would be here to suit the sex, *mestiça*.

[2] *Page* 99. Linschoten left Goa in November, 1588.

[3] *Page* 99. Also Belgam and Belgaon. It is the present Belgaum, about fifty miles west-north-west of Old Goa.

[4] *Page* 99. It is the rubies and sapphires only that are soft.

[1] *Page* 100. Pagode, or pagoda, was often used indifferently for the idol and the temple in which it stood.

[2] *Page* 100. "Buffle" is simply the French form—as "buffalo" is the Italian—of the original Greek *boubalos*; we have retained the Italian, but it has no philological superiority. Later in the text we shall meet the form "buf" or "buffe"

which gave us our "buff-coat", the complementary "skin" being dropped as in "kid-glove" for "kid skin-glove".

[3] *Page* 100. Gulconda is our Golconda. The Kutb Shahi dynasty reigned there from 1512 to 1688, and to Fitch and others like him in Golconda every King was simply Kutb Shah, just as in Bijapur he was Adil Khan—though wrongly —or Barid Shah in Bidar. The actual king of Golconda at this time was Mohammad Kuli Kutb Shah, who reigned from 1581 to 1611; he was succeeded by Abdullah Kutb Shah, who was the only Abdullah of his line. This is unfortunate, because without that name to be minced up and mixed into the wrong place it is difficult to account for the odd intruded "de la". We find Cotup Sha, Cuttuppsha and Coutou-Sha elsewhere, and there are probably many other strange forms, but the text form is the most surprising of all I have seen. The old royal fortress is still at Golconda, and great tombs of the ancient kings.

[4] *Page* 100. The last Bahmani King of the Deccan was slain in 1527 and his Kingdom split up, but for long a "King of Deccan" was spoken of still.

[5] *Page* 100. We should say now "of the first water"; the opposite phrase "of the new water" occurs later. Opals, turquoises and other such stones were said to be "of the old (or new) rock".

[6] *Page* 100. That is, the rainy season, which begins on this coast towards the end of May with the bursting of the south-west monsoon, and continues until about the end of September.

[7] *Page* 100. It is impossible to say whether or not Fitch actually went to Masulipatam (which, of course, is his "Masulipatan"). The "thence" in the next paragraph would logically indicate that he did so, but it is quite consistent with his easy-going style to take it as referring to Golconda. The fact that he does not say expressly that he went there is nothing; we find him later mentioning Satagam in much the same vague

fashion and discover that he certainly had been there. It is somewhere about three hundred miles from Golconda to Masulipatam, but judging from his care-free style of wandering that distance would be no deterrent to Fitch, while the port then lay in the Kingdom of Golconda, and therefore in reaching it the party would not have to leave the Mohammadan country in which they felt most at home (for Newbery spoke Arabic). On the other hand, Newbery's fidgety temperament might likely enough make him eager to press on to Akbar's Court at Agra, especially as he may have already formed the design of going on to Lahore and home through Persia ; in which case he would certainly see that there was no straying from the direct path. The point must be left doubtful, with a balance of probability against their having been to Masulipatam.

[8] *Page* 100. The "king of Bread" is certainly one of the Barid Shahi dynasty of Bidar ; the reigning King of the line at this time was Mirza Ali Barid Shah, 1572–1609. In the same way Fitch talks later of the "King of Samorin", intending the Samorin or Zamorin—the king of Calicut. "Servidore" is evidently "Shehrbidar"—"Bidar Town" ; the first member of which is the Persian *shahr* or *shehr*, a "village" or "town". Bidar is shown alternatively as "Beder" or "Cherbider" on Robert's map of 1751 and as "Shehr-Bider" on D'Anville's of the same date ; both are French, so the spellings are equivalent. Fitch says that they went to the "Country of Servidore", not the "town", so his phrase is akin to the modern conveyancing lawyer's "County of Southampton" (never, properly, "Hampshire"). The kinship is still more evident when we remember that Fitch would have written "country" instead of "county". The "country" of Bidar was then a belt of territory stretching up to the borders of Berar and probably called "Telingas" ; the party would naturally cross it, whether they reached "Bellapore" by way of Masulipatam or direct from Golconda.

NOTES

[1] *Page* 101. A sort of paste or plaster made commonly of wet clay, chopped straw or hair or something similar, and perhaps sand; it is used for plastering walls, making bricks, and for various purposes in various trades—for instance, moulds for metal-casting are made of it in some cases.

[2] *Page* 101. The present Balapur, six miles west of Akola, in Berar. It was an important place then and a natural point to make for.

[3] *Page* 101. Also spelt Brampore, Bramport, Brampour, Baramporte; the present Burhanpur on the Tapti river. It lay within Akbar's dominions but was not annexed by him until 1600. Before that it was ruled by princes of the Farukhi dynasty, the first of whom named it Burhanpur—" the City of Burhan "—after a famous Shaikh Burhan-ud-Din of Daulatabad. In the spelling " Brampore " note the same elision of an unaccented vowel as we have seen in " Bread " for " Barid ". It was famous for its cotton fabrics then and is so still. Ruins show that it once covered an area of five square miles—more than four times that of the old City of London, reason enough for Fitch to call it " marvellous great ".

[4] *Page* 101. Either the *mahmudi* or the *rupee*; both were round (some Indian coins were square) and thick and famed as good silver, but the *mahmudi* was worth twelve pence and the *rupee* twenty-seven. It almost looks as if someone had swindled Fitch over the exchange; about which he can have known very little.

[5] *Page* 101. These were Indian chintzes, from the Portuguese *pintado*, " painted ", and mostly designated by that word, though our early travellers frequently made strange work of it; " pentathose " and " pentathoes " are two of their efforts.

[6] *Page* 101. " Cotton-wool " is here woven cotton, not, as before, growing cotton or the substance we now call cotton-wool. Our first cotton fabrics came from the East, and of course through Italian hands, so it is natural for us to call them

(or their material) by the Italian name ; it was common practice in such cases. Now "*cotone mapputo*" (from "*mappa*", "cloth") was the early Italian name for cotton fabric and later Italians glossed it as "*cotone di lana*" ("cotton of wool", cotton-wool). There seems to be a mistranslation here, in the first place ; what was wanted was (coining a verb) "cloth-ed cotton", cotton made into cloth, but the Italians also lacked an explanatory verb for their old phrase and so we get our present "cotton-wool"—with a meaning totally different from its original one.

[1] *Page* 102. Spelt sometimes Mandowa, Mandow or Mandoa ; the present Mandogarh or Mandu. Once the capital of Malwa, it is now a place of splendid ruins. It was very strong, standing almost two thousand feet up on the crest of the Vindhyas and isolated by a valley four hundred yards broad and three hundred feet deep. The walls are said, with some authority, to have been thirty-seven miles round—certainly a "very great circuit". Akbar took it in 1570, but the twelve years' siege is a fable ; he never had to besiege a place even twelve months.

[2] *Page* 102. Ugini is nearer than our modern Ujjain to the original Ujjaiyini ; it stands on the River Sipra, was anciently the capital of Malwa and one of the seven sacred cities of the Hindus, and was taken by Akbar in 1571. Serringe is the present Sironj, in Tonk ; it was famous for muslins and chintzes.

[3] *Page* 102. Our Fatehpur-Sikri ; the old capital founded by Akbar in 1570 is now in ruins, which lie to the north-west of the present town.

[1] *Page* 103. Akbar was accustomed to give audience in the Diwan-i-Khas and judgment in the Diwan-i-Am ; "Derrican" may represent one of these.

[2] *Page* 103. Actually the distance is about twenty-four miles. By contemporaneous Mohammadan annalists it was

given as twelve *kos*; if Fitch heard of this and took the *kos* to mean a mile (as he very likely might) it would explain the mistake. The *kos* is about a mile and three-quarters. A sort of continuous bazar would be quite probable along a road constantly swarming with frequenters of the Court of every degree.

[3] *Page* 103. Merchants from all known parts of the Old World came to the great *sarai*, or inn, of Fatehpur in its great days.

[4] *Page* 103. The long muslin tunic still general in India. It is the Portuguese *cabaya*, probably from the Arabic *kaba*, "a garment".

[1] *Page* 104. Whichever.

[2] *Page* 104. Or Satagan (as he later calls it), Satgung, Satgoong, Satgong and Satigan, is Satgaon (properly Saptagram, "the seven Villages") thirty miles above Calcutta on the fork of the Hugli and Saraswati channels of the Ganges.

[3] *Page* 104. The Hindi *hing*, or asafetida, much esteemed in India, then and now, as a condiment, drug and perfume, in spite of its—to us—abominable taste and odour. Actually, many Europeans in India do consume asafetida—probably without knowing what it is; for, of very fine quality and in very minute quantities, it is used in the preparation of one of the accompaniments of their curries. It is a gum-resin prepared from the milky juice exuded by the cut-down stem of the plant *Ferula fetida*.

[4] *Page* 104. The Jumna.

[5] *Page* 104. This is the Sanskrit *yagnopavitam* or sacred triple cord of the Brahmans. It must be made of cotton gathered from the plant by a pure Brahman and carded and spun only by those of the Brahman caste. The three strands must become six and may become nine after the wearer's marriage.

[1] *Page* 105. Food in general, not flesh-food necessarily. We have just seen above that they eat no "flesh".

NOTES

[2] *Page* 105. A share or portion; still current in talking of common-rights, where it is used of the number of beasts a commoner may pasture.

[3] *Page* 105. The paste of sandal-wood; perhaps with saffron and other ingredients, but the sandal is the important thing.

[4] *Page* 105. "Ram, Ram", which is "God, God", is the usual salutation of two Hindus meeting outdoors. The "Grüss' Gott" of the Swiss peasant holds the same flavour.

[1] *Page* 106. Prag, Praga or Prayag was the ancient (and is the present) Hindu name of our Allahabad. Akbar gave it the new name about 1570.

[2] *Page* 106. Probably *Jogi* or *Yogi*; the Hindu ascetic or holy man of extremely variable holiness. Other old spellings are jaugui (by the French traveller Bernier, and so about equivalent to "zhogi" in our phonetics), chughi, and choki. But the word may be meant for *shaikh*, still a term for "priest" in Hindustani.

[3] *Page* 106. "A thing extraordinary", "a prodigy".

[4] *Page* 106. That is, the hair of their heads.

[1] *Page* 107. Benares. In other old travellers we have such forms as Bonarres, Bunnaroz, Bonares, and many more—all close enough to the original Sanskrit *Vanarasi* or *Banaras*.

[2] *Page* 107. Our "sash" began as "shash", and this passage appears to mark its first appearance in English. It was sometimes "shas", and from this last form, by a common letter-shift, attained its present spelling towards the eighteenth century. It is from the Arabic *shash*, "muslin", "turban-cloth", and is used in this sense by Fitch—not as meaning a sash for the waist. Benares was always famous for its turban-cloths, which were reputed better than any others.

[3] *Page* 107. "Parellel with", "alongside of"; a very usual form then, and belonging to the same corrupt kindred as, for instance, "amongst"—which we have retained.

[4] *Page* 107. These "straws" might be blades or stems of the sacred *Darbha* grass, *Poa cynosuroides*, or sprigs of the Holy Basil, *Ocimum sanctum*, or of one of the several other sacred plants of India.

[1] *Page* 108. Ada Maya is the goddess Lakshmi, the consort of Vishnu, in the capacity of Mother of the World; by certain of the Hindu devout she is exclusively worshipped as the symbol of the Eternal Being. Among her many forms she is shown sometimes with four arms, as Fitch saw her. The "great stone carved" is the *lingam*, the phallic symbol of Siva.

[2] *Page* 108. It is difficult to say whether this is the *Gyan Kup*—the Well of Knowledge—near the temple of Visvesvara, or the *Manikaranika* near one of the ghats. The *Gyan Kup* is a true well; the water is greenish and stinking with the quantity of marigold-flowers thrown into it, and it is very holy, for Siva is said to dwell there. The *Manikaranika* is a tank rather than a well; but steps lead down to it, it is much bathed in, the water is very foul, it receives its share of marigolds, and it, also, is very holy, for it is supposed to be filled with the sweat of Vishnu. Perhaps the *Manikaranika* just has it, but it is possible enough that Fitch had a confused notion of both places and described them as one.

[1] *Page* 109. The right side of the body, with its accompanying parts and members, has special attributes in Hindu religious ceremonial; it is, one may say roughly, the side of Heaven while the left is that of Hell. The ejection of water, for instance, from the left instead of the right side of the mouth in the course of ceremonial ablutions puts the ejector in grave peril of Hell.

[2] *Page* 109. A bell is commonly rung to attract the attention of the particular God to any offering which has just been made.

[1] *Page* 111. This marriage by the cow's tail is vouched

for elsewhere, and the cow appears frequently in the innumerable marriage customs of India. The Brahman mostly gets the cow.

[1] *Page* 112. The Sanskrit *Patana*, "The" Town, so more phonetically correct than our Patna. Patenau, Puttana, Pattana and Patanaw were some of the other usual early European spellings.

[2] *Page* 112. Possibly people of the Chuklar caste, or the robber-tribe of the Minas, who are likely to have been found at Patna; but these wandering tribes of thieves in India are beyond counting.

[1] *Page* 113. Patna became the capital of an independent state during Sher Shah's revolt against Humayun, Akbar's father, but Akbar took it again.

[2] *Page* 113. Tandan or Tanra was the old capital of Bengal after Gaur had ceased to be so. It was a very important city for nearly a century after Fitch wrote, but the Pagla offshoot of the Ganges on which it stood shifted its course—as Fitch says farther on—and the importance of the place passed. The name of it and some vague indication of its neighbourhood are preserved in the present petty village of Tanda, in the Maldah district of Bengal, but except that it was certainly near Gaur not even the site of the ancient city is exactly known. Gouren was of old the kingdom of Gauriya Bengala and Gaur, its capital, stood on a Ganges branch, but the waters drew away from it as from Tanda. The great ruins are somewhere over ten miles south of the present town of Maldah and have been excavated.

[1] *Page* 114. Couche is Kuch Behar—still thick with bamboos. Roughly, it is no more than a hundred and fifty miles from Tanda, direct, so Fitch evidently went there in his accustomed wandering and leisurely fashion. Suckel Counse appears to be Sukladuge, who certainly was a ruler of Kuch Behar, but what the "Counse" represents has so far eluded me.

[2] *Page* 114. Fitch entered Kuch Behar, but his knowledge of its farther boundaries is hearsay and so as tangled as a glance at maps of the time would lead one to expect. Hakluyt himself, in a marginal gloss, suggests that "Couche" is perhaps "Quicheu", that is, our Kwei-chau, and Fitch accepts this suggestion in his later mention of "Couche"; the distortion of the regions east of India seen in the old maps explains the feasibility of the idea. In this light, therefore, Kuch Behar and Cochin China might well have a common boundary, and "Cacchegate" may equally well be descended from "Kafchikue", an old Persian name (representing the Chinese Kiaochi-kwe) for Tong-King. If Tong-King is a country and not a port it does at least contain a notable port in Hanoi and a little more confusion among so much is no great matter for surprise.

[1] *Page* 115. Bitter almonds were common currency then, in some parts of India at least. They were of uncertain value, as one would expect such a money-token to be, but about sixty to the pice seems to have been the usual rate. The pice itself was a coin of extremely variable value, but it may be taken fairly correctly at something under a halfpenny.

[2] *Page* 115. The present Hugli; it was founded by the Portuguese in 1537. The latitude is exact.

[3] *Page* 115. "Dwell", "lodge", "abide"; you still "keep" in some certain part of a college at Cambridge.

[4] *Page* 115. Fitch's phrasing is amiably loose and might seem to suggest that it was Hugli the Portuguese called Porto Piqueno, the "Little Port"; actually it was Satgaon, to distinguish it from Chittagong, which was Porto Grande, the "Great Port". Satgaon had been the royal port of Bengal at least as early as the tenth century, and in the sixteenth was still a large trading city with many European merchants, but the Saraswati (which was then the main channel of the Ganges) began to silt up and the Portuguese founded Hugli to take its

place; the silting went on until Satgaon was left completely derelict. Now only some huts and ruins of a mosque and other buildings mark the spot, but its old life is shown by the remains of ships sometimes found many feet deep in the ground.

[5] *Page* 115. Direct, straight. We retain this sense in "go right ahead", also in "upright".

[6] *Page* 115. Angeli—or Hingeli, Ingelee and others—is Hijili, which is in Midnapur now but was in Orissa then. Sulaiman, the Afghan king of Bengal (the "King of Patan", that is, Patna), beat and killed the last Hindu King of Orissa outside Jajpur in 1568, but Akbar took the kingdom from the Afghans in 1578. Hijili is on the west of the mouth of the Hugli river, but in spite of frequent confusion the two names have nothing to do with each other. "Oriza" is the Portuguese form of Orissa.

[1] *Page* 116. Cloth made of "herba", "herbs", "grass" was said to be common in Orissa and thereabouts; it is still common in China and Southern India, made from quite different plants. This grass-cloth is what he means by "yerva" Such fabrics are found in many parts of the world.

[2] *Page* 116. May be from the Tamil *Chandai*, "a fair", or possibly he is remembering The *Chandni Chauk*, the open space where the market is held at Delhi, and using the wrong word of the pair.

[3] *Page* 116. An unusual spelling, but this seems to be meant for the Spanish *piraguas*, "dug-out canoes". Any kind of small boat was commonly meant by this much-corrupted word, some other forms of which are peroqua, periaqua, perriawger, pettyoager.

[4] *Page* 116. Deck.

[5] *Page* 116. The holy water of Ganges remains a miraculous specific for all ills, physical and spiritual. Pilgrims returning from Benares take it to the remotest parts of India in bottled portions properly sealed by a remunerated Brahman.

NOTES

[1] *Page* 117. "Tippara" is the modern Tipperah. "Chatigan" is Chittagong, called Porto Grande by the Portuguese. The "Mogores" would be the forces of the "Great Mogor", Akbar, under whose rule Chittagong ultimately fell. The "Mogen" were the Maghs (a Bengali name not recognised by themselves), the fighting race of Arakan; other old spellings are Mogs, Muggs, Moghs, Mogues, Mogos. Recon is the modern and less correct Arakan. The native name of the country is Rakhaing; the present corrupt form is apparently an Arabic version, "*Al Rakhan*", with the "l" of the article assimilated to the initial "r" according to rule. "Rame" is Ramu in the south of Chittagong; there is a modern town of Ramu in the locality. There were incessant wars between the Hindu King of Tipperah or Chittagong and the Buddhist King of Arakan, and they became rather worse than better when Akbar took Chittagong, until his Mughal governors of Bengal had thrashed the Arakanese into an uncertain peace.

[2] *Page* 117. "Bottanter" is our Bhutan. There is no city of "Bottia", though "Bhutesar" on the borders of Thibet is mentioned by Al Biruni, and the old cartographers show a "Badda" or "Bodda" thereabouts, but Bhutia is the correct name for the people of Bhutan, and as this was all hearsay Fitch may have mixed things. The spiritual ruler of Bhutan is the Shab-tung Rim-po-ché or Dharma Raja, evidently the text "Dermain"; like the Dalai Lama of Tibet, he is an incarnation of Buddha. The Bhutias are a short, stocky people, of typical Kalmuck appearance and build. It is possible that Fitch was told of, or had pointed out to him, some of the Kerantis, who are a tall strong race; their tract is rather to the westward of Bhutan, but they may have been as well-known in Cuch Behar at that day as they are in Darjiling now. The alternative is that "tall" here means "physically able"—a constant old sense of the word.

[3] *Page* 117. A coarse woollen cloth or blanket. Spelt in

all sorts of ways (cambolin, kummel, comley are a few of them), it is from the Sanskrit *kambala*, which is fairly close to our text.

[4] *Page* 117. The "high mountains" are the Himalayas and the "steep" one is Chumalhari, 23,949 feet.

[1] *Page* 118. The "Northern merchants" are Tibetans; the account of them which follows is accurate.

[2] *Page* 118. The tail of the Tibetan yak is cut off and made into the *chowrie* or whisk, still greatly valued in India and other Eastern countries for horse-trappings, fly-whisks, elephant-trappings and much beside. The "rump" is the short-haired piece of the cut-off portion—not what we commonly mean by rump. It is this sense of a short end or stump that the word holds in the Civil War "Rump" Parliament.

[3] *Page* 118. Bacola or Batticola is the present Barisal, about seven miles inland from the broad northern end of the Tetulia mouth of the Ganges and a little under twenty miles north of Bakargange.

[1] *Page* 119. In a certain previous edition of Fitch "Serrepore" was unhappily identified with the well-known Serampur on the Hugli river and near Hugli town; the point, therefore, must be discussed more laboriously than would otherwise be necessary. If a "Serampur" is needed there is one on the left bank of the Tetulia branch of Ganges, almost directly opposite Gaurnadi. This Serampur is about fifty miles from Sonargaon; allowing for the confusion between the *kos* and the mile, which I am persuaded was present in Fitch's reckoning of most Indian land-distances, this compares not outrageously with the six leagues or thirty-six miles (assuming the *kos*) of his hearsay distance, but to the Hugli Serampur the distance is just on a hundred and fifty miles—too great a difference to be accepted without explanation. The Tetulia Serampur is not much over twenty miles north of Barisal, along a continuous easy waterway, and so is a logical and convenient next stage; to the Hugli Serampur is a troublesome cross-country journey of

nearly a hundred and fifty miles. The Tetulia Serampur stands in a perfect maze of waterways, which cut up the country into innumerable islands; the neighbourhood of the other town is not noticeable for "many rivers and islands". Finally, down the Tetulia, inside Dakshin, across to the Meghna and out of it past Sandwip Island would be a perfectly natural course for the start of Fitch's voyage to Pegu; but to come out at the Hugli mouth, coast all along the Delta to Sandwip in the farthest eastern corner, and then turn about and go South on his determined course is the sort of perfectly idiotic thing no seaman would do without cause, and the cause would be either a foul wind or a port to be called at. Fitch mentions neither; proof positive as to the port, strongly presumptive as to the wind—the more so as he does trouble to mention the fair north-west wind which they did have. These geographical reasons are detailed not only because they must presumably dispose of the fixed legend of the Hugli Serampur, but because they equally support—if support is needed—the identification of the real Serrepore, which was not a "Serampur" at all. Misspelt also Seripore, Seeripore and Chiddipor, it actually was Sripur, a haven on the left bank of the Padma branch of Ganges, four miles south of Rajabari and just about forty miles from Sonargaon, which fits the text distance closely enough. It was a town important enough to give its name at one time to the Padma and to be identified tentatively with that mysterious old city of Bengala. It does not appear on modern maps because the Padma has shifted its channel about four miles north, so that Rajabari now stands on the left bank and Sripur lies somewhere in the bed of the river.

[2] *Page* 119. "Sinnergan" is the present Sonargaon, near the bank of the Meghna river fifteen miles east of Dacca. It is now in ruins, but was the ancient Mohammadan capital of Eastern Bengal until this was moved to Dacca in 1608. It was famous for its cloths and muslins.

NOTES

[3] *Page* 119. Isa Khan; at this time ruler of Lower Bengal, and in frequent revolt against Akbar. He died in 1598.

[4] *Page* 119. The Portuguese *fusta*, a vessel something below the average Arab dhow in size, but capable—as here—of fairly long voyages and of fighting.

[5] *Page* 119. Sandwip; to the East of the Meghna mouth of the Ganges. Famous for its salt.

[1] *Page* 120. From Bengal to Negrais by the shortest reckoning is not less than five hundred miles; it must be the *kos* again. "Negrais" is a European corruption of the Burmese Nagarit.

[2] *Page* 120. "Cosmin" is Kau-smin, the old Talaing name of what is now Bassein. This is probably the place he means, but it must be remarked that old maps show two other towns called Cosmin, one of them at the entrance of the Myaungmya river (by which I believe he travelled to Pegu), somewhere not far from the present Nga-pu-taw. Channels may have shifted, of course, but if he went to Bassein-Cosmin he would have to go twenty miles or so up the Bassein river and then down-stream again to turn into the inlet where the other Cosmin stood.

[3] *Page* 120. The average height of the Burmese proper is not quite five foot four, and all the other races of Burma are under this. Individually there are plenty of five foot eight and over, but "very tall" certainly does not describe the general impression; this is rather of stockiness, as in the case of the Gurkhas and Malays. The suspicion arises that Fitch employs "tall" in the frequent old sense of "physically able" generally, without reference to stature; a usage much resembling that of our present colloquial "stout fellow", which has no glance at adiposity. The engaging manners of the Burmese are famous. The women are an attractive golden colour, and unless Fitch uses "white" in the sense of "fair"—compara-

tively—he must have been deceived by their habit of powdering heavily. They do it very well.

[4] *Page* 120. These stilted houses are common throughout Farther India, not only as a protection against tigers, but for removal from water.

[5] *Page* 120. Or, as we should say, "where we make our landfall". The tip of the Arakan Yoma high hills runs down the middle of the peninsula of Negrais; the delta of the Irawadi—as he goes on to say—is the flattest alluvial plain, intersected by countless waterways.

[6] *Page* 120. Praus or prahus: spelt "prows" and in all sorts of other ways. A very well-known type of boat in Farther India.

[1] *Page* 121. The suggested identification of Medon with the modern Yandoon or Nyaungdon does not content me. The dissimilarity of the names is nothing in a country where, as I understand, every place has at least two native names as a matter of course, and where the European spellings of nearly all of them are hopelessly at sea. What seems entirely wrong about Yandoon is its position. Now whether Cosmin is Bassein or the other Cosmin at the mouth of the Myaungmya River, Yandoon is sixty or seventy miles inland from it to the north-east, and once at Yandoon it is a clear run of only about fifty miles to Syriam by a direct waterway. However leisurely and roundabout, therefore, the native boatmen may have been, it would seem too lunatic a proceeding for them to run back south-south-west seventy miles by the shortest route to reach Dala (presuming that the Dala of the old maps is meant and not the present Dala opposite Rangoon) and leave themselves still eighty or ninety miles from Syriam. Unless we, unreasonably, question Fitch's account altogether it is certain he went to Dala, and we know fairly well where Dala was. At a venture, then, I take Medon to be Myaungmya, which lies somewhere over ten miles from Ngaputaw up the Myaungmya

River, and the river leads across from Bassein River to Dala and has or had a Cosmin just within its western end some miles before you come to Myaungmya. Experts must decide whether the metamorphosis to "Medon" is impossible, but nothing of this kind appears to be impossible in Burma. If the present Dala is meant the argument, of course, collapses mainly, but then the old maps are more wrong than they have a right to be or we reason to expect. On all of them Dala is shown a long way from Syriam, whereas the present Dala is next door to it. Furthermore, Fitch should have seen the Shwe Dagon if he came down from Yandoon, yet he never mentions it till after he reached Pegu. The point cannot be stressed, as dusk or carelessness might account for the omission, but he would scarcely both reach Dala after sunset and leave it before sunrise—especially for so short a stage as that to Syriam.

[2] *Page* 121. Here, a big sunshade, as "umbrella" is a little sunshade. The one is the Spanish augmentative *sombrero*, from *sombra*, "shade", as the other is the Italian diminutive *ombrella*, from *ombra*, "shade".

[3] *Page* 121. There is a Dala on the bank of the river directly opposite Rangoon, but the old Dala stood at the inland end of the estuarial part of the Kyondon or Dala River. Fitch is explicit that it had "a fair port into the sea", and that is just how old maps show it.

[4] *Page* 121. Or Syriam, now Than-lyeng; it is six miles east of the present Rangoon, on the Pegu River near its confluence with the Rangoon River.

[5] *Page* 121. I take this to be Mayet-Kyi on the Pegu River, a little below Kawa and about thirty miles from Pegu. On Beckit's map of 1598 the waterways in this region are shown as a half-circle sweeping from Syriam to the sea eastward, with a straight stalk leading up to Pegu from the centre of the arc, a configuration which does in fact represent closely enough

the general arrangement of the Pegu River and the branch taking off from it below Dabein and running south and east into the sea at the mouth of the Sittang River; and on this map Macao appears in a position quite suitable for Mayet-Kyi. Thirty miles would be an easy day's journey by road, starting, as they would do, soon after sunrise in accordance with tropical custom. They evidently left the river here to avoid working up against the increasing force of the stream, a consideration which tells also against the Medon-Yandoon hypothesis. From Cosmin to Yandoon would be all up-stream work; from Myaungmya to Dala would be cross-stream by sluggish waterways with such currents as there were as much in their favour as against them. Burmese boatmen are certainly not the people to ignore this factor.

[6] *Page* 121. Also Deling and Delingo. A kind of hammock slung from a carrying-pole. A manner of conveyance widely employed in the East under many names, the origin of this particular name is uncertain, but very plausibly it is from the Persian *dalang* or *dilang*, "something suspended", or *dalingan*, "suspended".

[7] *Page* 121. A wooden bar or pole. To set an offender astride a pole carried shoulder high was a popular punishment called, in England, "riding the stang", in America, "riding a fence-rail"; "Huckleberry Finn" describes it vividly.

[1] *Page* 122. A warehouse or storage-place for goods in India and Asia east of India. Probably the Telugu *gidangi* through the Malay *godong*.

[2] *Page* 122. A far older phrase than "in a trice". To "trice" is to pull or hoist anything, particularly with a rope passed over a pulley, as sails are triced up; so that the phrase means "at one pull, or tug", hence "instantly". With the same central idea the French have "at a stroke", now represented by *tout d'un coup*, though once more closely by *à un coup*.

[3] *Page* 122. That is, for every side or face of the square.

NOTES

[1] *Page* 124. The Shawm or Shalm was an ancient wood-wind instrument which developed into the Hautboy, later, and now, called the Oboe. The word is from the Old French *Chalemie* or *Chalemelle*, which became *Chalumeau* after we had borrowed our "shalm". We have "shalmye" in Chaucer and "schallemele" in Gower—both very close to the French originals.

[2] *Page* 124. This would be about thirteen and a half feet. There is no record of an elephant of such a height.

[1] *Page* 125. This should evidently be "place", but it is "palace" in the original Hakluyt.

[2] *Page* 125. A fair description of the Keddah and what takes place in it. The "ointment" is not vouched for.

[1] *Page* 126. The *dah*, the national weapon of Burma and all these coasts. The true Kachin *dah* is about eighteen inches long, broad and square at the tip, narrow at the haft and sharpened only on one edge. It is a tool-of-all-work as well as a weapon and a symbol; venerated—by the Kachins, at all events—as the Japanese once venerated their sword, it is central in many ceremonies, is used to stir the wine in which an oath is pledged and is buried to mark the conclusion of a feud. Everywhere south of Bhamo the pointed *dah* of the Shans has become nowadays more fashionable than the square-ended form.

[2] *Page* 126. This may be the Sanskrit *suamin*, "Lord", used as a term of respectful address in South India, whence a good many locutions evidently travelled across to Burma.

[3] *Page* 126. Odia and, strangely, Judea were common early spellings of the present Ayuthia, Ayodhya or Yuthia, a Siamese town on the Menam, about forty miles above Bangkok. It was the Siamese capital for four hundred years until the Burmese took it in 1767. It is supposed that the place was called after the Hindu city Ayodhya, which is the present Oudh—a form not wonderfully different from Odia.

NOTES

[1] *Page* 127. Here, "a statue", a meaning the word "picture" retained until late in the eighteenth century.

[1] *Page* 128. Also spelt Maurian. With the meaning "a black person" we still retain this word in "blackamoor", where the "black" is redundant.

[2] *Page* 128. The fronds of some sort of palm—frequently the Palmyra-palm—are widely used in the East for writing or, rather, engraving, upon with an iron stylus about eight inches long. The traces left are faint, so, in Burma, a composition of charcoal and fragrant gum is smeared on, and when wiped clean the lettering is left distinct while the gum is a preventive of insect attacks; in India, less pleasantly, fresh cow-dung is the smearing-substance.

[3] *Page* 128. The old settlement of San Thomé, three miles south of Madras, was founded by the Portuguese in 1504. Its exports of *pintados* were famous.

[1] *Page* 129. Used. We "spend" time still.

[2] *Page* 129. *Sha* or cutch, *Acacia catechu*, which yields a valuable dye, brown turning to red.

[3] *Page* 129. That is, on the exchange.

[4] *Page* 129. Our Martaban.

[5] *Page* 129. From the Tamil *taragari*, a "broker".

[1] *Page* 130. Also ganza, gans, gance and others. Some kind of base metal used then in Pegu for small money. It is frequently mentioned by the early travellers and sometimes spoken of by them as lead, but although rough lumps of lead are still used in this way in the Burmese bazars gansa seems to have been something like brass or bronze; the word, at any rate, is the Sanskrit *kansa*, "bell-metal", through the Malay *gangsa*, which would be the form in current use caught by Fitch.

[2] *Page* 130. A corruption of the Tamil *visai*, by way of the Portuguese spelling *biça* and the Italian *byze*. It is a weight of almost three and a half pounds avoirdupois, and was later

called—correctly enough—the "viss" by foreigners in Burma, and by the Burmese themselves *peik-tha*, which the authorities say is probably still another corruption of *visai.*

[3] *Page* 130. From the context here and the usage elsewhere in the text "merchandises" might be expected, but it is "merchandise" in the original Hakluyt.

[4] *Page* 130. Or benzoin; the resin of *Styrax benzoin* and the incense made from it. Beijoim, benjuy and belzuinum are some other spellings, and the word comes, by a strangely devious road, from the Arabic *Luban Jawi*, "Java frankincense". Somebody thought the unaccented "lu" was the Arabic article; dropped it; ran the rest into one word, and we have our "banjawi" and all its strange variants.

[5] *Page* 130. Lacca or lac is the Hindi *lakh* from the Sanskrit *laksha.* It is a resinous substance which exudes from the Peepul and other trees when punctured by the Lac Insect, *coccus laccus.* In its crude form it is called stick-lac, in its final purified form shellac. Our word "lacquer" derives from "lac", as the substance is used in some kinds of lacquer. "Hard wax" describes lacca well enough in its stick-lac or shellac forms.

[6] *Page* 130. This may have been like the rice-wine of China, which is fermented with a yeast sometimes mixed with powdered dried fruits, sweet herbs, almonds and other things; it was esteemed very good drinking by Europeans and has been compared, in colour and a little in taste, to our modern Madeira. There is a coarser distilled spirit, made from rice or millet, sometimes called "arrack" but commonly "rice-wine", and the Burmese rice-wine may have been more like this.

[7] *Page* 130. Or Valera, Varelle and others. The name used by the Portuguese for the pagodas of Burma, Siam and countries east of them. Of doubtful origin, it may come from the Malay *barahla*, "an idol"; in this case, its use for the place in which the idol lived might have arisen through a mis-

comprehension by the Portuguese first hearers and is paralleled by the frequent old double use of "pagoda" for both temple and idol.

[1] *Page* 131. The Shwe Dagon—too often well described to need comment here. It is in Rangoon, which is about fifty miles from Pegu.

[2] *Page* 131. Spelt also talapoins, talpoys, tallopins and in several other ways. Until well into the nineteenth century the name used by Europeans for the Buddhist monks of Indo-China; properly known in Pegu as *phungyis*. The derivation is uncertain, but it seems to come from the Peguan *tilapoin*—*tala*, "lord", *poin*, "wealth".

[3] *Page* 131. A covered walk, especially one with shops at the rear of it. Any cloister or gallery, colonnaded or not, might have been called a pawn; the Pentice at Winchester, any of the London Arcades or the arcaded shops in Covent Garden are modern examples of what was once a pawn. The old Royal Exchange built by Gresham, and its successor built by Charles II, had lower and upper pawns, the upper pawn especially devoted to glove-shops, milliners, hosiers, haberdashers and such small commerce.

[1] *Page* 132. I take "kiack" to represent the Talaing *kyaik*, which begins the names of many pagodas and places famous for them in the Talaing district. Anywhere between Pegu and Sittang, or south of them, Fitch would be in this district.

[2] *Page* 132. Describes quite accurately the present wear of Buddhist monks in Burma.

[3] *Page* 132. This is evidently the Indian migrant *rawal* or *raul*, a "chief priest"; we have it in the present Rawal Pindi, "the village of the chief priest".

[1] *Page* 133. Rungs. In music, "staff" has the same visual suggestion; otherwise we mostly think of a staff now as something more or less vertical.

[2] *Page* 133. The traditional begging-bowl of the Buddhist; still carried, and called *Thabeit* in Burma.

[1] *Page* 134. Jamahey, or Saymey, is the present Zimmé—otherwise Maung Mai or Chieng Mai—on the Meh Ping river in North Siam. It is still the chief trading town of that country, and has large commerce with Burma through Moulmein and with China through Yün-nan. There are a good many hills between Pegu and Zimmé, but Fitch probably went along the coast south-easterly from Pegu, crossed the Salwin valley and river, went through the gap of the Dwana hills by the Moulmein trade-route and so across to the Meh Ping valley and up it to Zimmé; he would pass a lot of "very low" riverine country, as he says a little later, in travelling this way—which is the natural way, though roundabout. Chieng Mai lies roughly half-way down the belt of kindred peoples called Shans from Assam to Chieng Mai, and Laos from there onward to the borders of Cambodia. On the eastward edge of this part of the belt was the Laos state of Luang-Prabang in the Mekong valley, and this was called by Europeans Lanchan, Landjam, Lan John, Langianne and several other variants; while the chief town of the state was Jangomay, Zangomay, Jangoma and so forth, on the Mekong River. This makes it clear why Fitch used the alternative names.

[2] *Page* 134. The Shans are very much fairer than the Burmese—scarcely less fair than South Europeans.

[1] *Page* 135. Again, food generally.

[2] *Page* 135. The nuts of the Areca palm, *Areca Catechu*, used in compounding the famous betel or *pan* (usually miscalled betel-nut). The nut-kernels are sliced and dried in the sun; a small piece is rapped in a leaf of the Betel vine or *Sirih*, *Chavici betel*, together with a fragment of *chunam* or shell-lime and perhaps a dash of turmeric, cardamom or some other aromatic, and the whole is chewed—by perhaps a tenth of the human race.

NOTES

[1] *Page* 136. Now frequently spelt Capelan; seems to represent the native Kyatpin. The place is no longer the centre of the ruby-mining industry, which has shifted to Mogok.

[2] *Page* 136. The precious spinel or balas ruby is a crystal oxide of aluminum and magnesium; it is softer and less valuable than the true ruby.

[3] *Page* 136. Ava, on the Irawadi near Mandalay, was the capital of Burma from the fourteenth century to the eighteenth, and again for a few years in the nineteenth. It was destroyed by earthquake in 1839 and is still in ruins. Pegu and Burma were quite separate kingdoms at the time of our text.

[4] *Page* 136. The Burmese proper. Burma is shown on old maps as Brema, Brame and so forth.

[5] *Page* 136. This surprising custom is described by other old travellers. As no trace of it can be discovered now, and as the various accounts show a suspicious discrepancy in details, the authorities have finally concurred in dismissing the whole thing as a sailor's yarn. The remote foundation of the legend may be the custom, well known to exist among the Burmese and others, of inserting pellets of gold, coins, and different talismanic substances under the skin in order to produce invulnerability. If this really is the basis of the story, the boyishly obscene twist given to it is perfectly characteristic of the sailorman in all ages.

[1] *Page* 137. A cubit was anything from eighteen to twenty-two inches.

[2] *Page* 137. The male Burmese were and are accustomed to tattoo so profusely that they appear to be wearing a pair of skin-tight breeches.

[3] *Page* 137. A usual word for "pincers", "forceps", down to the seventeenth century; it is from the old French *pinçon*.

[1] *Page* 138. The black teeth are the result of betel-chewing. The "dog" idea was evidently an after-thought, something

like the fox and his famous tail; though there is a certain real feeling about it, since in French Indo-China, for instance, it is immodest for a woman to have white teeth, perhaps because the Frenchmen insist on them in any native ladies they favour.

[2] *Page* 138. Our Martaban, Tavoy, Tenasserim (the Islands of Tenasserim are those of the Mergui Archipelago) and Junkseylon or Salang.

[3] *Page* 138. Close, hard by. The Malays are still a proud people. It has been said of their warrior-swagger that they throw their shoulders about as if they belonged to somebody else.

[1] *Page* 139. The Moluccas; the Banda Islands lie about sixty miles south of them and almost until our time had the monopoly of nutmegs, as Amboina in the Moluccas had of cloves. Timor is the big island at the tail-end of the Lesser Sunda Islands east of Java.

[2] *Page* 139. That is, the Portuguese governor of Malacca, which was a Portuguese possession from 1511 to 1641, when the Dutch took it from them. We got it in 1825.

[3] *Page* 139. Achin, in the north of Sumatra. Always turbulent, it was never subdued by the Dutch until about thirty years ago and is not very much subdued now.

[4] *Page* 139. Macao had been a Portuguese settlement since 1586.

[5] *Page* 139. Better spelt "Carrack". The carrack was known in England at least as early as the reign of Henry V, but reached its greatest development as the chief type of merchant-ship in the sixteenth century, when the Portuguese carracks frequently ran to sixteen hundred tons, carried between thirty and forty guns and could accommodate a thousand souls or more. This was about the size of the *Madre de Dios*, captured by the English in 1592, and in 1594 the *Royal Exchange*, *Mayflower* and *Sampson*, of the Earl of Cumberland's fleet, destroyed the great carrack *Las Cinque Llagas*, of two thousand

tons and valued, ship and cargo, at £3,500,000 modern money. It illustrates the conditions of the struggle for the East Indian trade to mark that the English merchant-ships of the time often enough were of no more than a hundred tons, while one of four hundred tons, like the *Merchant Royal*, or six hundred, like Lancaster's *Dragon*, was reckoned a very big ship indeed.

[6] *Page* 139. The Portuguese coin *cruzado*, named so because it is "crossed"—marked with the sign of the cross, much like one of the English florins. The value varied with time and place, but might range from about four shillings down to two-and-fourpence, though in some cases it appears to have been worth as much as ten shillings.

[1] *Page* 140. This illustrates that mysterious "incachment" of which he speaks further on.

[2] *Page* 140. White is a sign of mourning in China; the "thread shoes" are the fabric shoes with thick soles worn in China still.

[3] *Page* 140. *Chunam*, or shell-lime. Used also in the preparation of betel.

[1] *Page* 141. Whatever the hair, this is still the writing instrument of the Chinese. Sometimes it is of cane, sharpened until it becomes a little brush of fibres at the point.

[2] *Page* 141. Labuan, off the north-west coast of Borneo, seems to be the nearest possible to "Laban", and Jambi in Sumatra to "Jamba"; but Jambi is not an island. As all this is what he had been told, however, exactness need not be looked for.

[3] *Page* 141 There is a small island, Bima, at the south-eastern corner of Sumbawa in the Lesser Sundas, but the description of labour customs applies too widely for certain identification. The Malays are lazy as well as "proud"

[1] *Page* 142. The South Indian form, *raya* of the Sanskrit *raja*, "a king", which gives also *rai*, *rao*, *rana* and various other dialect forms as well as the familiar "rajah".

[2] *Page* 142. In this place "naked" means "without body armour". The word was used in this sense at least as late as our own Civil War.

[3] *Page* 142. The attitude of formal courtesy not only in Ceylon but among many of the peoples of India.

[1] *Page* 143. Cingalese.

[1] *Page* 144. Cape Comorin. Comori or Comari, the usual old spellings, were more correct than Comorin, which is a Portuguese corruption of the Sanskrit *Kumari*, "a virgin", a title of the goddess Durga or Parvati.

[2] *Page* 144. Or, as we have it to-day, less correctly, Negapatam.

[3] *Page* 144. Or Kaulam, Kollam, Coilum, Colan and several other spellings; it is the modern Quilon. It is on the Malabar coast, which is eminent among all places for its pepper.

[4] *Page* 144. Elephantiasis is still prevalent in Ceylon and Southern India.

[5] *Page* 144. The Nairs are the polyandrous warrior race of Malabar. They wear their hair long and coiled on top of their heads.

[1] *Page* 145. A very light kind of matchlock that could be fired without a rest. It seems to be the same word as "calibre", and probably indicates that the weapon was of smaller bore than the harquebus.

[2] *Page* 145. "Hidden", as one would be in a closed litter. This word has been unaccountably missed by the Oxford English Dictionary. It is evidently from the French *cacher*. A little later than this Francis Drake, in his "Voyages", has "cache" from the same root, in its exact modern sense of "hiding-place", especially for food or treasure.

[3] *Page* 145. Custom, habit, fashion.

[4] *Page* 145. Stripped off or peeled. "Pill" and "peel" are merely variant spellings of the same root-word, and our modern form did not win the struggle for predominance until

the seventeenth century. The spelling "cinamom" seen here and elsewhere is less correct than our present "cinnamon"; the one represents the Latin "*cinnamomum*", whereas the other harks back directly to the original Hebrew "*kinnamon*".

[1] *Page* 146. For centuries "Zamorin" has been the title of the Hindu King of Calicut. It is the Sanskrit *samundri*, "the sea-king", through the Malayalam "*samuri*", other forms of which are "*samorim*" and "*zomodri*". Fitch evidently misunderstood his informant and took "Zamorin" for the name of a place, as he did in the case of the Barid Shahi.

[2] *Page* 146. The pirates of Malabar were of very ill repute from an early date until quite recent times. Their haunts dotted the coasts of Malabar, Kanara and the Konkan roughly from Cochin to Bombay, and not only the Portuguese but all other navigators of those seas were at constant strife with them. "Cogi Alli" is meant for Cogni Ali, which again is the Portuguese spelling of Kunbali, a great Mappilla (or Moplah) family of pirates in Malabar; they were fanatical Mohammadans. The Portuguese made the initial mistake in attributing the name of the family to their chief and Fitch followed the Portuguese

[3] *Page* 146. At once, instantly, impetuously. It occurs again in the next paragraph.

[4] *Page* 146. It is actually more like a hundred and forty leagues. Perhaps the *kos* was coming into his reckoning again.

[5] *Page* 146. Again his reckoning is out—this time to the extent of about twenty leagues only.

[1] *Page* 147. Until the flowers open the close-sheathed stem of the ginger plant, *Zingiber officinale*, does give it a certain distant resemblance to garlic.

[2] *Page* 147. Timor was generally reputed for its white sandalwood, which is *Santalum album*, to be distinguished from red sandalwood, or Sanderswood (sometimes, also, plain "Sanders"), *Pterocarpus santalinus*, an entirely different tree. The

paste of white sandal is part of the pigment used for tracing the various Brahman caste-marks and for various other ceremonial and toilet purposes ; with the addition of wood of aloes, saffron and musk it becomes *Chamva*, a fragrant ointment also used in the toilet.

[1] *Page* 148. The camphor of China is from a laurel, *Laurus* or *Cinnamomum camphora*, that of Borneo from a very big tree, *Dryobalanops aromatica* ; it was worth much more than the Chinese—a hundred times as much or thereabouts, it would appear. It was exported from Borneo packed in tubes of bamboo ; hence the common notion, indicated in the text, that it grew in canes.

[2] *Page* 148. Lign-aloes, aloes-wood or eagle-wood. The knots and heart-wood of the trees *Aloexylon Agallochum* (the best kind) and *Aquilaria Agallocha*. The resinous substance contained is prized as incense (its European medicinal use has been abandoned). It was called " sinking incense " because it sank in water, also " honey incense " The names are curious bits of corruption. The wood has nothing to do with " aloes ", which, in this case, is probably a perversion of the Arabic name *Al Ud*, " The Wood ", confused with the Greek *aloe.* " Eagle " is the Arabic *aghaluhy*, Malayalam *agila* ; by the Portuguese turned into *pao de aguila*, " aguila wood ", and then Latinised as *lignum aquilae*, " eagle wood "

[3] *Page* 148. Musk is a secretion of the gazelle-like musk-deer, *Moschus moschiferus*, found in the Himalayas and other Tibetan mountain systems ; it is contained in a gland by the navel. The gland is cut out, wrapped in a portion of the skin, dried, and so exported ; thus wrapped it is called a pod, or in earlier English a " cod ". If the gruesome mode of preparation detailed by Fitch (it is repeated elsewhere) ever was followed it was probably to disguise the adulteration with blood and meal freely practised by the Tibetans : it would account for any quantity of blood and mysterious foreign substances.

If it was a mere fable invented, as I suppose, by the Tibetans, it had to be—and was, in fact—accepted as truth by the outer world, for no one much but themselves knew anything about the matter. An alternative story was that the pure musk was so dangerously potent that for the protection of the users it had to be adulterated.

[4] *Page* 148. This is the ancient Vijayanagar in South India, seat of the great Hindu Kingdom of the same name. The text spelling is due to the Portuguese form "Bisnaga"; other spellings are Bicheneger, Bidjanagar and Bizenegalia.

[5] *Page* 148. The Portuguese *pescaria*, "a fishery". This was the name given by the Portuguese to the coast of Tinnevelly, from its great pearl-fishery.

[1] *Page* 149. This is the island of Hai-nan.

[2] *Page* 149. A substance frequently mentioned by travellers or commercial specialists of that and earlier ages, but exactly what is meant remains uncertain. The word means usually the product of incinerating vegetable matter or bone; ivory-black is an example. But from the accounts of other early travellers it appears that it may be applied to the metallic ash left when such substances as carbonate of zinc, sulphate of copper and others are treated in a furnace. Probably something like ivory-black is meant here; it would seem the more likely article of commerce.

[3] *Page* 149. Mardin, loftily placed on a spur of the Kurdistan highlands. It is here the great caravan-road from Baghdad branches, the northern fork leading on to Diarbekr and so to Constantinople.

[4] *Page* 149. Kurds. Cordies may be nearer the true spelling, for, according to Yule, one form of the name, Kordiaei, existed in this region before the Turkish language was known in it, so that a proposed derivation from the Turkish *kurt*, "a wolf", is impossible. The Persian *gurd*, "strong, valiant, hero", has been suggested as the root-word.

NOTES

[5] *Page* 149. Orfa is now spelt Urfah usually; otherwise Edessa. The Mohammadans believe that Urfah is Ur of the Chaldees and have Abraham's cradle there and his tomb (which is forbidden to Christian sight) and the Pool of Abraham, a great rock tank fed by a spring and swarming with Abraham's carp, as they believe them to be; this is the "goodly fountain". Actually, it was a pool consecrated to Derceto, the ancient Syrian fish-goddess, "Dagon" of the Bible.

[6] *Page* 149. Since leaving Baghdad he has been following the great caravan-road from that place to Aleppo. At Mardin it forks, the northern route going by way of Diarbekr, Sivas and Angora to Constantinople.

[1] *Page* 150. This is the "Daman" of Fitch; here it is spelt Portuguese-fashion.

[2] *Page* 150. The caravel was a smaller type of ship than the galleon or carrack, much used in the fifteenth and sixteenth centuries, especially by the countries of South Europe. The famous *Santa Maria* of Columbus was a caravel; she was three-masted, just over a hundred and twenty-eight feet extreme length, and of two hundred and thirty-three tons displacement fully laden. She was about the average of the type, but Vasco da Gama's almost equally famous *San Gabriel* was practically a caravel and she ran up to three hundred tons and had four masts.

[1] *Page* 152. "Ruin"

INDEX

Abilfada Ismael (Abulfeda), 38 and *n.* 2

Aborise (Abu Risha), 68 and *n.* 1, 71

Abowsher, Abushahr (Bushire), 51 and *n.* 1

Abraham, 149 and *n.* 5

Acacia catechu, *n.* 2 to p. 129

Achen, Achem (Achin), 129, 139 and *n.* 3

Achillea ageratum, *n.* 1 to p. 67

Ada, 108 and *n.* 1

Adil Shah, *n.* 6 to p. 78

Affection, 31 and *n.* 4

Agra, 76, 102, 103, 104, 106, 114, 116, 148

Agulias, Cape das (Cape Agulhas), 23, 26

Albatross, *n.* 8 to p. 23

Albocore (albacore), 25 and *n.* 4, *n.* 1 to p. 26

Albuquerque, Mathias de, *n.* 1 to p. 60, 74, *n.* 3 to p. 91

Aleppo, 37, 38, 39, 40, 45, 46, 48, 49, 50, 51, 52, 55, 60, 61, 62, 63, 65, 67, 68, 70, 79, 82, 84, 85, 89, 90, 97, 99, 104, 149

Allen, Ralph, 48, 49, 51

Almains, 79 and *n.* 1

Almonds as money, 115 and *n.* 1

Aloexylon agallochum, *n.* 2 to p. 148

Alongst, 107 and *n.* 3

Angeli, Hingeli, Ingelee (Hijili), 115 and *n.* 6, 116

Antioch, 68

Antonio, Don, 60 and *n.* 2, 62, 79, 81

Antwerp, 82

Aquilaria agallocha, *n.* 2 to p. 148

Arabia, 29, 68, 71, 72, 73, 90

Arabians, 44, 45, 68, 70, 71, 72, 112

Archbishop of Goa, 81, 82, 94, 95

Areca Catechu, *n.* 2 to p. 135

Armenia, 71

Arrecaes, 135 and *n.* 2

Artemisia absinthium, *n.* 1 to p. 67

Asafetida, *n.* 3 to p. 104

Asmerome, Arziron, Alzarome, Carztron (Erzeroum), 39 and *n.* 1

Ava, 136 and *n.* 3

Aveador General, 80 and *n.* 4, 81, 82, 83

Aynam (Hai-nan), 149 and *n.* 1

Azores, 23

Babel, Tower of, 45, *nn.* 1 and 2 to p. 46, 72 and *n.* 1

Babil gehenham, 67 and *n.* 3

Babylon, Babilon, Bagdet (Baghdad), 34 and *n.* 3, 38, 40, 45 and *n.* 2, 46, 47, 50, 51, 52, 54, 56, 61, 63, 65, 66, 67, 68, 70, 71, 72, 73, 86, 149

INDEX

Bacola, Batticola (Barisal), 69, 118 and *n.* 3, 119
Badu, Sultan, 75 and *n.* 7
Bagala, *n.* 3 to p. 58
Baharem, Baharim (Bahrein), 58 and *n.* 6, 73, 74, 148
Balsara, Balsora, Baçora, Basora, Bussorah (Basra), 34 and *n.* 4, 38, 40, 41, 48, 49, 50, 51, 52, 53, 54, 55, 56, 58, 59, 60, 61, 62, 63, 64, 66, 72, 73, 86, 147, 149
Banda, 139 and *n.* 1, 147
Bannaras, Bonarres, Bunnaroz, Bonares (Benares), 107 and *n.* 1, 112
Bardes, Bardez, 96 and *n.* 2, 97
Barrampore, Brampore, Bramport, Brampour, Baramporte (Burhanpur), 101 and *n.* 3
Barret, William, 40 and *n.* 2, 42, 48, 68
Basaim, Bazim (Bassein), 76 and *n.* 4
Bassa (pasha), 38 and *n.* 5, 55, 56
Bate, Anthony, 68
Batman, bateman, 51 and *n.* 5, 53
Bazar, to make, 63 and *n.* 3, 64
Begging-bowl, 133 and *n.* 2
Beholding, 32 and *n.* 1
Being, 19 and *n.* 3
Bellapore (Balapur), 101 and *n.* 2
Bellergan, Belgam, Belgaon (Belgaum), 99 and *n.* 3
Bengala, Banzelo, Bemgala, Banghella (Bengal), 69 and *n.* 1, 100, 102, 104, 106, 113, 114, 115, 116, 118, 120 and *n.* 1, 129, 142, 144, 148
Benjamin, beijoim, benjuy, belzuinum (benzoin), 130 and *n.* 4, 135, 148
Betel, *n.* 2 to p. 135
Bethlehem, 68
Bets (Leedes ?), William, 83
Bima, 141 and *n.* 3
Birrah, Bira, Bir, Birra, Biredjik, Birejik, 43 and *n.* 1, 44, 70, 71, 149 and *n.* 6
Bisapor (Bijapur), 78 and *n.* 6, 99
Bisnagar, Bicheneger, Bisnaga, Bidjanagar, Bizenegalia, 148 and *n.* 4
Biza, 130 and *n.* 2
Borassus flabellifer, *n.* 5 to p. 30
Borgers, Bernard, 82, 94
Borneo, 129, 148
Bostocke, Thomas, 42
Bo'sun Bird, *n.* 3 to p. 24
Bottanter (Bhutan), 117 and *n.* 2
Bottia, 117 and *n.* 2
Bow, to, 24 and *n.* 3
Bramanes (Brahmans), 104, 105, 111
Bramas, 136 and *n.* 4, 137
Bread, King of, 100 and *n.* 8
Bridge of boats, 47 and *n.* 2, 71
Bristow (Bristol), 35 and *n.* 7
Bruges, 82, 92
Brush-writing, 141 and *n.* 1
Buffle, buf, buffe, 100 and *n.* 2, 103, 114, 115, 134
Burning Zone, 21 and *n.* 1, 24

Cabie, 103 and *n.* 4
Cacchegate, 114 and *n.* 2
Cadie, 64 and *n.* 1

INDEX

Caffyls, caffylen, 90 and *n.* 1
Cafre, 30 and *n.* 1
Cairo, 41
Calecut, kalyko, calocowe, callaga, 58 and *n.* 2
Calendar, old reckoning of, 57
Calicut, 144, 145
Calivers, 145 and *n.* 1
Cambaia, Cambaietta, Cambeth, Cambaet, Khambat (Cambay), 31 and *n.* 3, 59, 69, 75, 76, 77, 116, 128, 144, 149
Cambals, cambolin, kummel, comley, 117 and *n.* 3
Camphora, 129, 148 and *n.* 1
Canaria, Great, 20
Canarian Isles (Canary Islands), 20
Canton, 139
Cape Sheep, *n.* 8 to p. 23
Caplan (Capelan), 136 and *n.* 2
Captain of Ormus, 60 and *n.* 1, 62, 74, 75, 79, 80, 81, 83, 84, 86, 91
Carack, 139 and *n.* 5, 144
Caravallos, Albert, 119
Caravel, 150 and *n.* 2
Cargason, 42 and *n.* 1
Carsies, 48 and *n.* 1, 49, 50, 63
Cauchin China, 114 and *n.* 2, 141, 148
Cave, 55 and *n.* 4
Cayro, cairo, cair, cayar, kiar, 73 and *n.* 1
Cento, 55 and *n.* 2, 65
Certify, 19 and *n.* 2
Ceylon—*see* Zeilan
Chandeau, 116 and *n.* 2
Chatigan (Chittagong), 117 and *n.* 1, 118
Chaul, 76 and *n.* 6, 86, 87, 146
Chavici betel, *n.* 2 to p. 135
Cheap, 49 and *n.* 1, 88
Chekin, sequin, zecchin, 84 and *n.* 3
China, 117, 118, 129, 134, 138, 139, 140, 141, 148, 149, 151
China, King of, 32, 59
Chingalayes, 143 and *n.* 1
Chonderi, 69 and *n.* 2
Chondery, 119
Chownam, 140 and *n.* 3
Chowrie, *n.* 3 to p. 54, 118 and *n.* 2
Churle, 53 and *n.* 3
Cinnamon, cinamom, 51, 53, 54, 65, 143, 145 and *n.* 4
Cirion, Syriam (Than-lyeng), 121 and *n.* 4, 129
Cloves, 51, 53, 54, 65, 81, 147
Cochin, 69, 78 and *nn.* 4 and 5, 142, 144, 146, 147, 150, 151, 152
Cocos (coco-nut), 30 and *n.* 6, 120, 121, 135, 144, 145, 146
Cogi Alli, 146 and *n.* 2
Columbo, 142
Comori, Comari (Comorin), 144 and *n.* 1
Compass, variation of, 23 and *nn.* 5 and 6
Conclude, 19 and *n.* 4
Conduct, 54 and *n.* 1
Cordies, Curdi, 149 and *n.* 4
Cosmin, Kau-smin (Bassein), 120 and *n.* 2, 129, 141
Cotton-wool, 36 and *n.* 3, 101 and *n.* 6, 116, 143
Couche (Kuch Behar), 114 and *n.* 1

INDEX

Coulam, Kaulam, Kollum, Coilum, Colan (Quilon), 144 and *n.* 3
Coverture, 116 and *n.* 4
Cow-dung, 77 and *n.* 3
Cravancera, 55 and *n.* 4
Crusadoes, 139 and *n.* 6
Cubit, 124, 137 and *n.* 1
Curna (Kurna), 57 and *n.* 2
Currall, 41 and *n.* 2
Cutch, *n.* 2 to p. 129
Cutup de lashach, Cotup Sha, Cuttuppsha, Coutou-Sha (Kutb Shah), 100 and *n.* 3

Dah, *n.* 1 to p. 126
Daman, Damaon, 76 and *n.* 3, 150 and *n.* 1
Damasco (Damascus), 38 and *n.* 7
Danec, 43 and *n.* 3, 72
Deal, 40
Deccan, 100 and *n.* 4
Deceived, 91 and *n.* 2
Defend, 56 and *n.* 2
Dela (Dala), 121 and *n.* 3
Delingeges, deling, delingo, 121 and *n.* 6
Delli, Dilli, Dehli (Delhi), 76 and *n.* 1, 116, 148
Dermain, 117 and *n.* 2
Derrican, 103 and *n.* 1
Diamonds, 91, 99, 100, 103, 139, 141, 148
Diego, Frey, 150
Diu, 75 and *n.* 2, 76, 86, 87
Dogonne, 131 and *n.* 1
Downs, The, 40
Drake, Francis, 80 and *n.* 3, 81
Drette, Rue, 80 and *n.* 2
Dryobalanops aromatica, *n.* 1 to p. 148
Ducat, 41 and *n.* 4, 42, 48, 51, 53, 62, 63, 64, 78, 87, 88

Ears, perforated, 74 and *n.* 5, 114, 117, 143, 145
Ecebar, Ekber (Akbar), *n.* 2 to p. 31
Egyptian (gipsy), 44 and *n.* 3
Eldred, John, 34, 43, 47, 51, 57 59, 61, 64, 66
Elephantiasis, 144 and *n.* 4
Elephants, white, 123, 124
Elephant-trapping, 124 and *n.* 2 to p. 125
Elizabeth, Queen, 31, 32, 58
Emanuel, The, 40, 41, 48
Emeralds, 84
Enkhuisen, 82
Equinoctial, 21 and *n.* 1
Euphrates, River, 43 and *n.* 2, 44, 57, 67, 70, 71, 72, 73, 149

Falmouth, 38, 40
Fast, 138 and *n.* 3
Fatepore (Fatehpur-Sikri), 102 and *n.* 3, 103, 104
Feathers, 54 and *n.* 3
Felugia, Feluge, Feloge, Feluchia (Felluja), 43 and *n.* 5, 45, 50, 52, 70, 71
Fernandez, Francis, 38 and *n.* 4
Ferula fetida, *n.* 3 to p. 104
Fitch, Ralph, 34, 39, 48, 49, 59, 69, 83, 85, 88, 89, 99 seq.
Flux, 28 and *n.* 1
Flying-Fish, 25 and *n.* 1 to p. 26
Foist, 119 and *n.* 4

INDEX

Fondeghi Ingles, 35 and *n.* 1
Forked Tails, 24 and *n.* 3
Franks, 55 and *n.* 1, 56
Fusse, 65 and *n.* 2

Gagara, jaggery, 76 and *n.* 8
Ganges, River, 69, 106, 107, 112, 114, 116 and *n.* 5, 119
Gansa, ganza, gans, gance, 130 and *n.* 1
Garde, 24 and *n.* 5
Gaza, 68
Gentiles, 74, 75 and *n.* 5, 77, 79, 100, 101, 102, 104, 105, 107, 114, 115, 116, 118, 151, 152
Ghufa, *n.* 1 to p. 47
Gill, George, 52
Ginger, 51, 53, 65, 147 and *n.* 1
Goa, 19, 27, 30, 31, 38, 56, 59, 60, 62, 65, 69, 75, 78 and *n.* 3, 79, 81, 85, 86, 88, 89, 90, 92, 96, 97, 99, 146, 147
Gobar, *n.* 3 to p. 77
Godon, 122 and *n.* 1
Gold, 112, 122, 124, 127, 130, 131, 135, 139, 141, 148, 150
Good Hope, Cape of, 20, 21, 24, 26 and *n.* 2, 27
Gouren, 113 and *n.* 2, 115
Governor (steersman), 29 and *n.* 4
Grass-cloth, *n.* 1 to p. 116
Gratify, 32 and *n.* 2
Gravesend, 37
Great Canaria, 20
G.S., 47 and *n.* 3, 61, 64
Guillame, Peter, 39
Guinea, 20
Guinea Ship, *n.* 3 to p. 21
Gulconda (Golconda), 100 and *n.* 3
Gyan Kup, *n.* 2 to p. 108

Hakluyt, Richard, 37 and *n.* 4
Hamburgh, 81
Hammah (Hamah), 36 and *n.* 2
Hareborne (Harborne), William, *n.* 3 to p. 47, 50 and *n.* 1, 54
Heit, Ait, Is (Hit), 67 and *n.* 2, 72
Hell door, 67 and *n.* 3
Hercules, The, 69
Hidalcan, Adil Khan, Adil Shah, 78 and *n.* 6, 100
Hinge, 104 and *n.* 3
Hoise, 22 and *n.* 1, 26
Horse trade, Indian, 74 and *n.* 3, 75
Hospitals, animal, 78 and *n.* 1, 115
Hugeli (Hugli), 115 and *n.* 2

Idols, 100, 107, 108, 109, 110, 111, 123, 127, 128, 130, 131
Incached, *n.* 1 to p. 140, 145 and *n.* 2
Indico, 58 and *n.* 1
Indies (and India and East Indies), 19, 27, 28, 29, 38, 40, 41, 46, 48, 49, 51, 53, 56, 69, 70, 73, 75, 78, 83, 88, 90, 92, 93, 100, 103, 113, 116, 119, 128, 138, 139, 144, 147, 150, 151
Instantly, 34 and *n.* 1
Ipomoea Turpethum, *n.* 1 to p. 53
Isacan, 119 and *n.* 3
Italy, 19

INDEX

Jaffa, Joppa, 42, 68, 69
Jamahey, Saymey, Imahay (Zimmé, Maung Mai, Chieng Mai), 69 and *n.* 3, 134 and *n.* 1
Jamba, 141 and *n.* 2
Jangomay, Zangomay, Jangoma, *n.* 1 to p. 134
Jangomes, 134 and *n.* 1
Janissary, 35 and *n.* 5, 37, 58, 68
Japan, 139, 141
Jaugui, chughi, choki, *n.* 2 to p. 106
Javas, 139, 141, 148
Jemena (Jumna), River, 104 and *n.* 4, 106, 114
Jerusalem, 42, 68
Jesuits, 19 and *nn.* 5 and 6, 28 and *n.* 3, 81, 92, 93, 95, 96, 98, 151
Jeweller, the—*see* William Leedes
Jones, Philip, 39
Jordan, River, 68
Junsalaon, Junkseylon, Salang, 138 and *n.* 2

Keep, 115 and *n.* 3
Kelek, Kelleg, 47 and *n.* 1, 71
Kiack, 132 and *n.* 1, 133

Laban, 141 and *n.* 2
Lacca, lac, 130 and *n.* 2
Lace, 30 and *n.* 4
Lahore, 104
Lakshmi, *n.* 1 to p. 108
Lanchan, Landjam, Lan John, Langianne (Luang Prabang), *n.* 1 to p. 134
Langeiannes, 134 and *n.* 1, 136
Larine, larin, 84 and *n.* 3
Larus canus, *n.* 3 to p. 24
Laurus (Cinnamomum) camphora, *n.* 1 to p. 148
Leaves, writing on, 128 and *n.* 2
Leedes, William (the Jeweller), 49, 70, 96, 104
Leese, 56 and *n.* 1
Leg, standing on one, 142 and *n.* 3
Lewdly, lewd, 51 and *n.* 4, 53
Libanus (Lebanon), 35, 36
Lignum Aloes, lign-aloes, aloes-wood, eagle-wood, 148 and *n.* 2
Linscot, John (Linschoten, Jan Huyghen van), *n.* 1 to p. 30, 82 and *n.* 1, 89 seq.
Lisbon, 19, 23, 85, 150
Loam, 101 and *n.* 1
Locks, 74 and *n.* 4
Lycia, 68

Macao, 139 and *n.* 4
Macao (Mayet-Kyi), 121 and *n.* 5
Maces, 51, 53, 147
Madagascar, *n.* 1 to p. 27
Madera (Madeira), 20 and *n.* 1
Magdalene, Maudlin, Sweet Maudlin, 67 and *n.* 1
Magnetic variation, 23 and *nn.* 5 and 6
Magosine, 55 and *n.* 4
Mahmudi, *n.* 4 to p. 101
Main, 26 and *n.* 4
Maine, 22 and *n.* 1
Malabars, 143, 144, 146
Malacca, 69, 90, 116, 119, 121, 138, 139, 141, 150
Malacca, Captain of, 139 and *n.* 2
Malayos, 138 and *n.* 3

INDEX

Maluco, Moluccoes, Malucos (Moluccas), 80 and *n.* 3, 81, 139 and *n.* 1, 147
Mandavi, River, *n.* 2 to p. 89, *n.* 2 to p. 96
Mandoway, Mandowa, Mandow, Mandoa (Mandogarh, Mandu), 102 and *n.* 1
Mangas de Velludo, *n.* 3 to p 24
Manikaranika, *n.* 2 to p. 108
Maravedi, *n.* 3 to p. 42
Marriage customs, 101, 105, 111 and *n.* 1
Martavan (Martaban), 129 and *n.* 4, 138, 141
Mascarenhas, Don Francisco de, 75
Masulipatan (Masulipatam), 100 and *n.* 7, 128, 129
Meat, 78 and *n.* 2, 105 and *n.* 1, 115, 135
Mecca, 77, 121, 129, 139
Mecca, Straits of, 75 and *n.* 3
Medine, madyne, maydin, medin, 42 and *n.* 3, 51, 53, 71
Medon, 121 and *n.* 1
Merdin (Mardin), 149 and *n.* 3
Meneses, Don Gonsalo de (Gonçalo de Menezes), 91 and *n.* 3
Messe, 62 and *n.* 3
Mestizo, 99 and *n.* 1
Mogen, Mogs, Muggs, Moghs, Mogues, Mogos, 117 and *n.* 1, 120
Mogor, the Great, 69, 76, 102, 113
Mogores, 117 and *n.* 1
Monster, 106 and *n.* 3
Moors, 30 and *n.* 3, 74, 75, 76' 77, 79, 90, 101, 102, 104, 107' 116, 149, 150, 152
Morian, Maurian, 128 and *n.* 1
Mosambique, 27
Moschus moschiferus, *n.* 3 to p. 148
Moscovites, 79
Mosul, 46 and *n.* 3, 149
Mouth of Hell, 72 and *n.* 3 to p. 67
Muscovia, Moscovia, 117, 118
Musk, 54, 114, 117, 130, 139, 148 and *n.* 3
Muttons, 66 and *n.* 1

Naires, Nairs, 144 and *n.* 5, 146
Naked, 142 and *n.* 2
Nandi, *n.* 3 to p. 77
Nastrayne, Nostrane, Nazaranie, 51 and *n.* 3, 53, 79
Naucrates ductor, *n.* 1 to p. 25
Neel, 53 and *n.* 2
Negapatan, 116, 144 and *n.* 2
Negrais, 120 and *n.* 1, 129
Newbery, John, 31, 33, 34, 37, 39, 42, 43, 48, 49, 50, 52, 54, 58, 59, 61, 62, 63, 65, 70, 79, 89, 96, 97, 104
Next, 22 and *n.* 2
Nineveh, Ninive, 46 and *n.* 3, 149
Nizam-ul-Mulk. *See* Xa-Maluco
Norfolk, *n.* 3 to p. 47, 49
Nutmegs, 51, 53, 65, 147

Oak-galls, 36 and *n.* 4
Occam, 58 and *n.* 4
Odia, Judea (Ayuthia, Ayodhya, Yuthia), 126 and *n.* 3

INDEX

Order, 145 and *n.* 3
Orfa, Urfah (Edessa), 149 and *n.* 5
Orient, 73 and *n.* 2
Orixa (Orissa), 115 and *n.* 6, 116
Ormus, 50, 53, 54, 55, 56, 58, 59, 60, 61, 62, 63, 64, 69, 70, 73, 74, 75, 77, 79, 80, 82, 83, 84, 85, 86, 87, 89, 90, 91, 99, 147, 149
Osborne, Sir Edward, 60 and *n.* 3, 62, 70
Overseen, 26 and *n.* 3
Ozeah (El Ozeir), 57 and *n.* 1

Padre Mark (Marco), 82 and *n.* 2, 86, 87, 92, 95, 98
Pagode, 100 and *n.* 1, 123, 127, 128, 131
Painter, the. *See* James Story
Palmer, pawmer, 76 and *n.* 9, 78, 122, 144, 146
Palm-tree, 30 and *n.* 5
Palm-wine, 30 and *n.* 6, 77 and *n.* 2
Palmyra-palm, *n.* 5 to p. 30
Pardau, pardawe, pardao, 80 and *n.* 1, 84 and *n.* 3, 94, 97, 98
Paroes, prows, parowes, 120 and *n.* 6, 121
Patamar, 97 and *n.* 1
Patan, 115 and *n.* 6
Patenaw, Patenau, Puttana, Pattana, Patanaw (Patna), 112 and *n.* 1, 113 and *n.* 1
Pawn, 131 and *n.* 3
Pearl-fishery, 144, 148 and *n.* 5
Pearls, 54, 73, 74, 90, 91, 103, 148, 150
Pegu, 69, 100, 104, 118, 119, 120, 121, 124, 128, 129, 130, 131, 134, 136, 138, 139, 141, 143, 148, 150
Pepper, 51, 53, 54 and *n.* 2, 100, 114, 116, 117, 129, 130, 139, 144, 145, 147, 148
Pericose, peroqua, periaqua, perriawger, pettyoager, 116 and *n.* 3
Persia, 38, 39, 51, 53, 63, 64, 71, 73, 74, 90, 103, 104, 117
Persia, Gulf of, 73
Pestered, 86 and *n.* 1, 120
Peter, Frey, 150
Phaethon, *n.* 3 to p. 24
Physalia Pelagica, *n.* 3 to p. 21
Picture, 127 and *n.* 1
Pike, 84 and *n.* 4
Pilled, 145 and *n.* 4
Pilot-Fish, *n.* 1 to p. 25
Pinjrapol, *n.* 1 to p. 78
Pinsons, 137 and *n.* 3
Pintadoes, pentathose, pentathoes, 101 and *n.* 5, 128 and *n.* 3
Piper longum, *n.* 2 to p. 54
Piper nigrum, *n.* 2 to p. 54
Piper officinarum, *n.* 2 to p. 54
Piscaria, 148 and *n.* 5
Plat, 62 and *n.* 1
Point (of Africa), 22 and *n.* 3, 23 and *n.* 4
Poore, Leonard, 39, 52, 79, 85
Porter, Edmund, 42
Porter, Giles, 42
Porto Grande (Chittagong), 117 and *n.* 1, 119
Porto Piqueno (Satgaon), 115 and *n.* 4
Porto Santo, 20 and *n.* 1

INDEX

Portugal, 19, 30, 74, 78, 80, 81, 92, 93, 95, 96, 144
Portugals, 20, 24, 59, 74, 75, 76, 78, 115, 139, 142, 144, 146, 151
Portuguese Man-o'-war, *n.* 3 to p. 21
Positor, 84 and *n.* 2
Prage, Prag, Prayag (Allahabad), 106 and *n.* 1
Presently, 146 and *n.* 3
Promontory (Cape of Good Hope), 21, 22
Propriety, 24 and *n.* 2
Pterocarpus santalinus, *n.* 2 to p. 147
Purchas, Samuel, *n.* 3 to p. 47, 50
Pusillane, puselen, purcellain, purselane, 65 and *n.* 4

Quarter-point, *n.* 5 to p. 23
Quicheu, *n.* 2 to p. 114, 117

Raia, 142
Rama, 68
Rame, 105 and *n.* 4
Rame (Ramu), 117 and *n.* 1
Rated, 41 and *n.* 5
Rea, Francis de, 82
Recon (Arakan), 117 and *n.* 1
Red Sea, 29, 139
Remembrance, 83 and *n.* 2
Remora brachyptera, *n.* 2 to p. 25
Respected, 95 and *n.* 2
Reynolds, The Bark, 41
Rice-wine, 130 and *n.* 6
Right, 115 and *n.* 5
Right side, 109 and *n.* 1
Road, 36 and *n.* 1
Rotello, rotola, rotilo, rotula, rottula, rottil, rottel, ratlo, 49 and *n.* 4, 53
Rowli, 132 and *n.* 3
Rubies, 91, 99, 103, 127, 130, 136, 143, 148
Rump, 118 and *n.* 2
Rupee, *n.* 4 to p. 101
Rushtails, 24 and *n.* 3

Saia (sha), 129 and *n.* 2
St. George's Island, 34
St. Laurence, Isle of, 27 and *n.* 1
St. Michael, Island of, 23
St. Paul, College of, 59, 81, 82, 86, 87, 95, 98, 99
Samorin, Zamorin, 146 and *n.* 1
Sandals, sanders, 76 and *n.* 7, *n.* 3 to p. 105, 129, 147 and *n.* 2
Sanderson, John, 50
Santalum album, *n.* 2 to p. 147
San Thomé, 128 and *n.* 3, 129
Sapphires, 99, 127, 130, 136, 143, 148
Satagam, Satgung, Satagan, Satgoong, Satgong, Satigan (Satgaon), 104 and *n.* 2, 115 and *n.* 4, 116, 117
Scarlets, 49 and *n.* 3, 129
Schesche, 106 and *n.* 2
Scrivano, 83 and *n.* 1
Scurvy, 27 and *n.* 1 to p. 28
Seen into, 91 and *n.* 1
Selwy, 137
Serion, Serrion, 133, 140
Serrepore, Seripore, Seeripore, Chiddipor (Sripur), 119 and *n.* 1
Serringe (Sironj), 102 and *n.* 2

INDEX

Servidore, Cherbider, Beder, Shehr-Bider (Bidar), 100 and *n.* 8
Set forth, 70 and *n.* 1
Several, 35 and *n.* 2
Shales, William, 48, 49, 51, 59, 61, 64, 66, 68
Shans, *n.* 2 to p. 134
Shashes, 107 and *n.* 2
Shawmes, shalm, 124 and *n.* 1
Shemines, 126 and *n.* 2
Ship of Guinea, 21 and *n.* 3
Shivering, shiver, shive, 58 and *n.* 5
Shold, 43 and *n.* 4
Siam, 69, 126, 136, 148
Signior, the Grand, 50 and *n.* 2, 55
Silk, 51, 53, 76, 103, 114, 116, 117, 118, 139
Sinnergan (Sonargaon), 119 and *n.* 2
Skinner, William, 48, 49, 51
Sodden, 28 and *n.* 5
Sodom, Sea or Lake of, 68 and *n.* 2
Sombreros, 121 and *n.* 2, 132
Some, 65 and *n.* 1, 71
Spain, King of, 60, 62, 152
Spaniards, 56, 57
Spent, 129 and *n.* 1
Spinels, 127, 130, 136, 143, 148
Spodium, 149 and *n.* 2
Spoil, 152 and *n.* 1
Sport, 96 and *n.* 1
Stang, 121 and *n.* 7
Staper, Richard, 41, 60 and *n.* 3, 62, 70
Staves, 133 and *n.* 1
Stevens, Thomas, 19 seq. and *n.* 1, 38, 59, 78, 82, 86, 87
Stevens, Thomas (Father of Thomas Stevens, the Jesuit), 19
Still, 77 and *n.* 1
Stilted houses, 120 and *n.* 4, 133
Stint, 105 and *n.* 2
Story, James (the Painter), 49, 59, 62, 70, 82, 87, 93, 98, 99
Strappado, 89 and *n.* 1
Stroopenny, Stropene, Stropennie, Michael, 54, 60, 62, 79, 80, 84 and *n.* 5
Styrax benzoin, *n.* 4 to p. 130
Suckel Counse, 114 and *n.* 1
Sucking-Fish, *n.* 2 to p. 25
Sue, 87 and *n.* 1
Sumatra, 100, 116, 119, 121, 129, 139
Sundiva (Sandwip), Island of, 119 and *n.* 5
Suttee, sati, 77 and *n.* 5, 110
Swarve, 23 and *n.* 6, 29
Syndye, Cinde, Sindu, Scinde, Cindy (Diul-Sindi), 54 and *n.* 3

Taborer, Andreas, 88
Tallipoies, talapoins, talpoys, tallopins, 131 and *n.* 2, 132, 133, 134, 135
Tana (Thana), 76 and *n.* 4
Tanaseri (Tenasserim), 138 and *n.* 2
Tanda, Tandan, Tanra, 113 and *n.* 2, 114
Tapestry, 74 and *n.* 2
Tareghe, 129 and *n.* 5
Tari, *n.* 5 to p. 30
Tattooing, 137 and *n.* 2
Tavi (Tavoy), 138 and *n.* 2
Teeth, black, 138 and *n.* 1
Tenerif (Teneriffe), 20

INDEX

Tibetans, 118 and *n.* 1
Tiger, The, 34, 48, 52, 70
Tigers, 26 and *n.* 5, 103, 106, 114, 115, 119, 120
Tigris, River, 46, 47, 57, 71, 72, 86, 149
Timor, 139 and *n.* 1, 147 and *n.* 2
Tippara (Tipperah), 117 and *n.* 1, 120
Tipperdas, 113
Toddy, *n.* 5 to p. 30
Trapezunde, Trabisonda (Trebizond), 39 and *n.* 1
Trice, 122 and *n.* 2
Tripolis (Tripoli), 34 and *n.* 2, 36, 38, 40, 68, 69, 70, 89, 149
Tropic Bird, *n.* 3 to p. 24
Tuberone, tiburon, tiberune, 24 and *n.* 4
Tuition, 39 and *n.* 3, 42
Turband, 65 and *n.* 3
Turbetta, turbith, turpeth, turbit, 53 and *n.* 1, 54
Turkia, 71 and *n.* 1
Turks, 36, 58, 71, 72, 73, 79, 90

Ugini (Ujjain), 102 and *n.* 2
Use, 44 and *n.* 1, 118
Uttered, 95 and *n.* 1

Varellaes, valera, varelle, 130 and *n.* 7, 131
Variation of Compass, 23 and *nn.* 5 and 6
Velvet Sleeves, 24 and *n.* 3
Veneseander, venetiander, 98 and *n.* 1
Venetians, 36, 54, 55, 62, 63, 90, 91, 99
Verde, Capo, 20
Viceroy of Goa, 56, 62 and *n.* 2, 75, 78, 80, 81, 87, 88, 92, 94, 96, 97
Vintem (vintin), *n.* 1 to p. 30
Vizrea, 62 and *n.* 2

Warner, Walter, 39
Water, old and new, 100 and *n.* 5, 141
Worms, 21 and *n.* 2
Wormwood, 67 and *n.* 1

Xa-Maluco, Zemelluco, 76 and *n.* 6

Yerva, 116 and *n.* 1

Zecchiah, 57 and *n.* 1
Zeilan, Sailan, Selonc, Seilan, Ceilon (Ceylon), 69 and *n.* 3, 119, 142, 144, 145, 146, 149
Zelabdim Echebar, Yeladin el Kubar (Jalaluddin Akbar), 31 and *n.* 2, 58, 69, 101, 102, 104, 113 and *n.* 1, 116, 119
Zindi (Sind), 75 and *n.* 1
Zocotoro, Sacatora, Secutra, Socotera, Scotra, Sechutera, Sokotora (Socotra), 29 and *n.* 1
Zone, Burning, 21 and *n.* 1, 24

Treasure of Books

Under One Roof

Demand Any Rare Book at

www.facsimilepublisher.com

Demand Any Rare Book at:

www.facsimilepublisher.com

if not available, give information,
our team will search and update you.

Promote Knowledge:

If you have any rare book
which is not available at
www.facsimilepublisher.com,
offer it to other readers so that others can also be
benefitted with your cooperation.
The book will be printed with your courtesy.

Print & Publish:

If you wish to get your book printed or published,
we have the service for you.

Customization on Demand:

We offer customization of books
as per the demand of the customer.

Published by

Facsimile Publisher
Ashok Vihar, Delhi-110052 (India)
Website: www.facsimilepublisher.com

Distributed by

Gyan Books Pvt. Ltd.
5, Ansari Road, Daryaganj, New Delhi-110002 (India)
E-mail: books@gyanbooks.com, Website: www.gyanbooks.com

2 222000 011888